Circle of Memories
(Alpha and Omega)

Circle of Memories (Alpha and Omega)

A Book of Original Poetry

Silvio Q. DellaGrotta

VANTAGE PRESS
New York

FIRST EDITION

Published by Vantage Press, Inc.
516 West 34th Street, New York, New York 10001

Manufactured in the United States of America
ISBN: 0-533-11391-1

Library of Congress Catalog Card No.: 94-90847

0 9 8 7 6 5 4 3 2 1

To my wife, Mary, who has walked beside me with unselfish devotion and gentle understanding

Contents

Preface

Man is a creature of emotion. He is as changeable as the weather. The tempest flashes across his mind with more swiftness than gliding clouds. It comes ánd perhaps stays awhile, making its disturbance felt within the heart. And while the storm rages, the mind envelops itself in darkness and brooding. Out of the subsequent turmoil, man loses hope and has little faith in the future. The whole pattern of life becomes a matrix of melancholia, bitterness, distrust, and despair.

Then, as the storm loses its fury, man sees a ray of light. Like the sun breaking through the clouds, all of the futility begins to evaporate and in its place a sliver of hope glows. Man grasps at this flicker and his heart surges and pounds. He looks up from the pit of despair toward the skies. His lips form a prayer. His heart loses its load; the blood streams faster. Life begins to have a ray of hope.

Finally the clouds vanish and the sun shines forth in all its brilliance. Man stands as though naked beneath the warmth and glory of the light. He stands erect and casts proud eyes at the world about him. Everywhere there is hope.

And so man passes through the cycle unscathed, a trifle stronger and with faith in the future.

This book of poems seeks to present man in his varied moods and passions, his hates, his loves, his despairs, his hopes, his wishes and his dreams. The poems run the gamut of emotion.

Some of the poems are filled with hope. Some have an undercurrent of faith. A few are desolate and melancholy. But all the poems are part of the tapestry—a mosaic of man's life.

Acknowledgments

To the optimists of the world who subdue their daily travails and persist in unending quests for goodness in fellowmen.

To the pessimists that furrows are erased from their brows if they discover serenity is theirs for the taking.

To the world that each of us will accept the other with a sign of peace and friendship, and the reach of a loving hand.

To friends who share dreams and aspirations, and whose concerns and kindness inspire warmth and gratitude.

To husbands and wives everywhere that they will acknowledge their vows of commitment and pursue life as one with untarnished trust and unflinching faith in each other walking hand-in-hand in harmony to their happy rewards.

To Rose Mary Asuncion, whose commitment, belief in the author's work, proficiency, and computer skills brought the manuscript to life and whose dedication to the work involved afforded the author the ease of review.

Circle of Memories
(Alpha and Omega)

Prologue

Hope*

Hope is a seed within the mind,
A flower in the heart,
A prayer borne in the soul.
If you do not plant that seed, the flower
Will not flourish and the prayer is muted.
Hope is the soft whispers of a springtime breeze,
The rustle of the late autumn leaves,
The white purity of the new winter snow.
If you stifle the whisper and the rustle
Or 'smirch white snows, then hope is destroyed too.
Hope is the soft glow of the morning star,
The first twinkle of the evening star,
Or the sheen of full moons on placid lakes;
It is the refreshment of the aurora,
Or the delicacy of the painted dusk;
It is the kiss of a raindrop on thirsty earth
And the sparkle of dew caught by the sun.
Hope is an herb to salve the pains of life,
A wine to stun the mind of its fight,
A food to sate the hunger of the heart,
A medicine to resolve the uneasiness of being;
Hope is the threshold of salvation,
The flicker to dispel darkness of defeat,
The beacon to inspire one to ride out the storm,
The torch to lead the way for dreams to come true.
Hope is many things—
A wistful sonnet, a lover's dream,
The remembrance of a tender kiss,

* Extracted from "Of Derelicts and Diamonds" by the author

A soft embrace, a caressing hand;
It is the lullaby of a mother to her child,
The regret of a meeting ended all too soon;
It is the dream of the future closely fondled,
It is the memory of moments nostalgic—
Aye, hope is many things.
Hope is the mirage of better things to come,
The yearning for life to bear its fruits;
It is the entrance into tranquillity,
The doorway to a peaceful garden,
The fragrance of a budding rose;
It is the bustle of the busy bee,
The scurrying of the anxious ants,
The contentment of a little calf,
The purr of a kitten, the cry of a crow,
The agitated bark of a dog for its master,
The whistle of a train far off in the night,
The glow of light to guide travellers in darkness,
The flutter of a flag rising in the dawn,
The emotion in the heart upon thoughts of home.
Hope is the seed and the flower of life,
The key to the doorway of ambition and desire,
Destroy hope and you destroy faith,
And without faith man is lost forever.

Faith

Faith is a flower
    That grows 'neath a light of hope;
Faith is refreshment
    Drawn from the deep well of a soul
    To quench the agony of despair and fear;
Faith is the fire
    That chars cobwebs of confusion;
Faith is the power
    To bring eruptions of strength,
    To wither ramparts of depression.
Faith is the desire
    To fill joy's cup to its brim.
Faith is the starlight
    That brings much peace of mind
    While casting off the fears of the day.
Faith is the contentment
    Without bounds or restraint.
Faith dispels darkness
    As the sun lights the morn
    So never lose faith—
    A gift tried and true
    Beckoning ever for use by you.

Charity

Charity can prevail
If mankind would allow.
Charity is the act of love
The offer of one's heart.
Charity is a chalice
Filled with unselfish gifts
For the destitute of spirit.
Charity is the art of giving
Not expectations from life.
Charity is a flower of mercy
A bouquet given to sinners.
Charity is spirituality of being
Unfettered, endowed freely.
Charity is beyond an act of alms
It is generosity of faith
    Prayers for atonement
    Chastity of thought
    The gift of giving:
    Aid to the suffering
    Uplifting victims of life
    Forgiveness to all.
Charity has no limits,
It spans time and space
Selflessly given it can free
The world's human race.

Book One

Vanity

Vanity

Youth fueled dreams to
  Conquer the world
So that passersby would turn
  Their heads to proclaim
There is an achiever
  Above the crowd
  Who has it made.

At midlife the passion
  For thunder is muted
Need for adulation in embers
  Survival for self-esteem
And self-respect paramount.
  No need for travelers to turn
Their heads and proclaim
  Paeans of one's glory.

Upon reflection o'er days
  Of a lifetime
Youthful dreams did conspire
  To create grand illusions
In lieu of consuming struggle of one
  Gripped in jaws of stark reality.

When I was young, there was
  A burning fire to conquer life
So that passersby would turn
  Their heads to say:
There's one who has everything
  He's above the crowd
  He has it made!

When I reached mid-life
    Passion for thunder was gone
Need for adulation in ashes
    Survival in daily toil paramount
No need for passersby to turn
    Their heads for praise,
There was no cause for such.

At eventide of life
    Reflective of days of yore
Lessons learned from boyhood dreams
    Conspired to create half a man
Who failed to conquer himself
    Through faith in reality.

Uninvited Guests

Life has many facets,
Some rare and some fine,
Others deathly and sad,
Wicked, darkened or bad.
Life depends upon the one
Who looks into its depth
Or seeks its pleasures
While others weep and sigh.
Life can be marvelous,
Bringing forth great joy,
Swelling one with success,
Filling another with wealth.
But life can be morose
With humans failing to gain
Serenity of mind or soul,
Struggling toward vague goals;
And life can freeze man,
Moving neither forward or back,
Rooting himself to evil
And sinking into hell.

What is this thing, life?
All have different views
Concerning its significance
And all that it denotes.
What treasure does life hold?
Some say it has much wealth
To fill the beating heart
With a miraculous stealth.

How does life progress?
Each follows a different path
That has varied destinations
Of arts and science and crafts.
Where does this life lead?
Perhaps to golden heaven,
Or maybe to depths below
Where souls remain unleavened.
And why is there life?
Some think it a weary trial,
A tribulation and a burden
Filled with anguishing cries.

Life is what one lives,
Making of it what one wills,
Reaching for the heights
Or diving into dank pits,
Life is filled with cunning,
One must be ever on guard
Or be swallowed by black demons
From which no escape lies.

Life may be filled with joy,
The brightness of good cheer,
The mellowness of fine years,
Or the wonders of sweet hours.
Yes, life is what one makes it
And some face it with spirit
While others are defeated
From the moment of their birth.
And life is beyond one's control,
None asked to be born into it,
We come as uninvited guests
With no future except death.

The Newcomer

We looked at you and smiled;
You saw not yet, tiny and full,
But we knew you understood;
Asks one: but how? such a babe
Newly entered through the veil
Of life, bereft of recognition
Knows. Foolish are those who
Stand not on the other side
Of the door and gaze at this
New spark of life—this divine
Gift which rends sorrow
And brings great content to hearts.
How can I tell you, son,
What passed between us that day
We first saw you clutching
At the nurse who held you to view?
Just a threshold separated us
And soon you would cross it
Into the outer world to grow
Into a man. What awaits you?
Your mother and I know not
Of course, but years of plans
Have now found the source
Upon which to play and cause
And no matter what the years
Ahead contain, our thrill
Was to see you born, to touch you
The first time. And as we fade off
Into the haze of years, my mind,
And Mother's too, shall recall
That hot summer day when your

Wail portended a new life
Upon wretched Earth. We shall know
Other thrills as we watch you grow;
For all our efforts are directed
Now to the days you give us—
Each filled with new treasure,
Untold wealth, to be cherished
In hearts long burning for
A newborn son. I write these
Few lines with a smile,
A tender smile, for only forty-eight hours
Have passed and yet I can envision
The sturdy boy, the anxious youth,
The mature man.
I wished I could reach out that day
To hold you, but impatience is an evil;
The days to come many times
Shall I reach out to steady
Your course, but with patience,
Until that day when my hand
Will falter and you reach out yours,
And then I'll know that baby boy
I loved so very much
Is a man.

When We Were Ten

The second hand sweeps across the face
Of the clock that hangs upon the wall;
Time flees before its implacable will
Swift as the hunted before the hunter;
And we watch the clock while minutes pass
With vague hopes life will forever last,
But unimpeded flees time as we gaze
While footsteps falter and eyes glaze.

When we were ten towards 'teens we looked,
Wishing that time would forge ahead;
And when they came we looked beyond
To moments when we reached the prime;
Too soon the spring of youth passed by,
And agility of mind slowed to a pace,
Stairways heightened, footwalks lengthened,
And time etched faces with weariness.

The time soon comes to dare look back
To the fleeting days of the age of ten,
And old hearts yearn they were back again
To visit the dreams and hopes they held;
Yet fascinated by the sweeping hand are we
As without remorse it moves steadily on,
Pushing us towards that very last moment
When no longer for us will there be time.

If I Were a Little Boy Again

If I were a little boy again
I'd dream of Mother fair,
Of her sweet and gentle voice
And her loving tender care;
I'd recall her soothing smile
Her laughter and her cries,
But most of all I'd remember
The love shining in her eyes.
My mother was not beautiful
Some said not even pretty,
But God never made a mother
Finer than He gave to me.
I still feel the tender warmth
As I nestled in her arms
Where her caress of sureness
Guarded me from all harm.
Stardust glistened in her hair,
Sunlight blessed her smile,
Heaven never shone as bright
As love-tears in her eyes.
I remember funny fairy tales,
Lullabies murmured to me,
Oh! if I were a little boy again
How different I would be.
The dear Lord gave me a mother
And placed me in her care;
Blessed was I with a mother
Pure as the heavens fair.

If I were a little boy again
I'd fill her cup with joy,
Never utter an unkind word
And act like her little boy.

The Common Man

This is the story about a man,
Not a man of fame, fortune or renown
But a simple, ordinary man
Taken up with turmoils of daily life,
Who passes, unnoticed by fates,
Which spur a man and raise him high,
This is not a story of events,
Or wastrel cast in fool's luck,
Or soldier ribboned with honors,
Or genius called on for advice.
It is a recitation of a frail soul
Who comes upon the earth to strive
For many things yet achieves few
But who in his placid travel
Touches others with his presence.
This is the story of a serene man
Who daily struggles for the bread
To give to those who fill his life
With love and other little things
More valued than gold or gems;
A man who finds his kingdom lies
Not beyond the fantasy of dreams
But within the confines of his heart
With those who bless him with love.
He is a quiet man
A citizen of highest order
With love for his country
And love for his God
And love for his family;
Who appreciates his neighbors
And his charity to unfortunates

Deprives him of small luxuries;
He is the summary of all men
Who place their faith and trust
In the knowledge life cannot
Everyone with gilded wand touch
Nor shower affluence, nor jewels,
But he understands, and therein
Finds the magic of the treasure
That makes him the common man.
This is the song of any man
Who justly finds that he
Donates a little of himself
Every day, and in this giving
Receives a little of someone else;
Nor passively, nor tempestuously
Through the passageways of life
But who defines his circumstance
And then proceeds without incident
Until his task is done;
This is the paean of a man,
A simply ordinary common man
As you and I?
Who speaks not with fancy words
Nor composes symphonies or schemes
Who yearns for many things
But is satisfied with less,
Who sometimes wonders at himself
Yet understands his limitations,
Who dreams ofttimes of fineries
But who finds comfort in his life.

The Omnipotent

Look at me! You laugh now,
But there was a time when men feared.
I see the derision in your eyes:
Once subjection would rule there.
Ah! time wreaks peculiar tricks
And man becomes warped and bent
Beneath the weight of kismet
And the treachery of the years.
Who would have dared to scorn
A year or two ago?
Who would have pointed a finger
At someone who was strong?
Strong . . . no, there is weakness now,
There is no strength to lift men
Into a web of servitude—
There is no longer the force
To show men who is boss.

To recapture that past glory—
That could be my aim,
But the fear is the reign is done
And I must slip away
Into a vacillating pose
Deadly abhorrent to such as I—
To such as I . . . well have I lived,
Not in the light of fellowman,
For some say that I lived
By ruining the weaker ones
Who came across my path.
And yet my actions were not meant
To retard any. Were they strong as I,

Then I would have been vanquished
And tossed off to the lions,
For strength knows no foe save strength.

Mortal am I though
And as all men must someday go,
The power has dissolved
Like jelly beneath steam . . .
Steam of time dissolves everything
Since no abutments can man build
To ward off the corrosion
Which gnaws at its tired foe.
And yet I live in my dreams,
Nor can I forget that once
Time was but an insolent thing
That could not deter me.
Little did I reckon with its power—
It was so much more potent than I
As I learned all else could I conquer
Except time which would make me die.

Were I to live this life again
I know what I would do:
I would make plans accordingly
And consider time in all my schemes.
But I suppose my schemes would differ
And to accumulate wealth and such
Might prove of little consequence
Whenever I thought of death's touch;
Instead I would apply my power
To pave the path for those who follow,
That perhaps they too might see
The knowledge which came to me:
    The equalizer is not one's power

Because one day that shall go,
Instead it is the comprehension
Of what makes a fellowman of foe.

Where Gaily Sings the Bird

Tranquillity lies upon a plot of ground,
A plot covered with deep sod;
The sod is green
And on it did perch
A little bird that gaily sang
Its song of peace and quiet.
And on that sod the sun did shine
With knowledge of nothing wrong;
But nowhere is there peace on earth
Except when man reverts to dirt,
Finding his home within the ground
While the world goes round and round;
And man may wish that he too
Were beneath that sod,
That sod so green
Upon the plot
Where the bird so gaily sang.

The jester cried, "That is no bird
That sits on tree or sod,
The song you hear
Depends on the ear
As you make of life what you will:
A sedate trip or boisterous flight,
Filled with anger or fun
To the end hope's victory is won.
For where you travel in this sphere
Man lives with much hope and fear.
Seeking an eden of success on the ground,
Within a world of cruelties' bounds;
And man in his dreams

Surveys the world's scene,
That arena of strife,
Of tumbling life
Where he plots and plans and schemes."

"Nay!" cried one at all this despair,
"The bird sat on a tall tree;
The tree was alive
With vibrant life
And his song the gay bird sang,
A song of hope and promise.
And below that tree life did pass
Fulfilling fine dreams and desires.
For where over earth you may go
There live men with strong hope
Looking for improvement on the ground
While the world totters round and round;
And man in his hopes
Is raised atop the tree,
That tree so tall
With vibrant life
Where the bird so gaily sang."

'Tis hope that drives us all
Toward goals beyond our reach
Constrained by the daily turmoils
Besieging our plans and schemes.
Yes, 'tis hope which reigns supreme
To illumine limits of our dreams.
'Tis hope that scatters vile turns
Which seek to ravel our concerns.
Unsought, one day, the ragged covers
Of our book of life will close,
No more for us will there be hope

As man is placed beneath the sod,
The sod is green
Upon the plot
Where the bird will gaily sing.

An Old Man Dreams

Frost curls o'er this aged head
Rime mists my fading eyes,
Memories surge into my mind
As sadness stings my heart.
Well do I remember all
The halcyon days of youth
When spring blossomed sweet
And laughter swept the blue.
Long nights come, short days go
Lost swift in earthly quest
Of bygone time when golden sun
Gave warmth to edenic rest.
Ah, spring! Wouldst that I
Could rumble once again
'Neath the chaste purity
Of perfumed April rains
Or smell the buds of springtime
Aburst on stately trees
With hearty zest and fervor
Of youth careless and free.
Alas! These flighty forays,
Mere promenades of the mind
Are born of wishful thought
E'en as years my body bind.

Contemplation

Death may be my lot, as death to all men comes
And though the somber thought pricks my mind
Yet eager heart beats on in worth of life;
And though my breath shall be stilled
No more to cloud frosty winter air,
Or take in the sweet scents of spring,
My journey shall carry me through the hours
Until one day my head will rest forever
On satin nothing, still and cold and gray.

    Until then I need reflect on better things
    Which one by one occurred, a tapestry formed
    By sublimal artist deep within
    The delicate canvas of the mind
    Emblazoned memories ne'er washed away;
    A beauteous enduring masterpiece,
    A magical work of art time cannot erase
    A miracle aglow on sturdy museum wall.
    Thus I bask within contented gaze of mine
    Turned inward to my mind, reveling each moment
    This arras sublime, and then reweave anew
    Into another miracle finer than before.

The hoary thoughts of eternal quiet flee
Even as the past years cast weight unseen
Upon aging body sapped by earthly trials
Molding graying head and wrinkled brow.
What better refuge than redolent haven
Where repose tender morsels of life?
Fear of the unknown trek need must flee
As vigor regenerates the fount' of youth

To rekindle the thrills of happier days
Which again meander through paltry flesh.
Alas, indeed! That life must be curtailed,
But hasten back while life endures,
Gaze through shadows into dim horizons,
Recall the artifacts of a mind e'er enriched
By the artistry life granted to it.

Indeed, my head shall rest no more to move
And my heart no longer beats within my breast
And beauty once affluent in riches' glory
Will be shuttered. Still life the sweeter was
For bestowing gifts of pleasant hours
Poured from golden cups to gild my mind;
And more, perhaps my journey into outer lands
Shall be illuminated by what in life was mine.

Death

Death! Such terror grips the heart
When its meaning mantles it.
The mind in revulsion flees in haste
Seeking refuge in a brighter place.
But death begins on the day of birth.
Without concession to any man.

Some shudder and in desperation reach
For sedatives to disband gloom so deep,
Which moccasins the inevitable end;
So, without reconcilement with fate,
They think it possible to make death wait.

But the wise man is ever the one
Who knows one day he shall expire,
Resigns himself to his destiny of doom,
Prepares himself without fear or gloom.
He knows no struggle he may stage
Can leave death helpless in futile rage.

So he lives his plans in much accordance
Without fighting his end discordant.
Thus, his life grows in peaceful content
He does not succumb to senseless fright
Thereby banishing sorrow by day and night.

My Guardian Angel

My child sleeps;
The deep, sweet slumber of peace,
Silent, eternal, and tranquil;
She is gone from me—
My child sleeps.

She slumbers
In deep silence she rests,
Mid echoes of her footsteps,
While I walk these ways alone,
My child sleeps.

Just yesterday it seems
Her laughter rang,
Her voice gaily spoke words
Or I chided her
For frivolous acts.

Now . . . now, all is quiet,
A shroud of silence reigns,
And I seek to part
The curtain of sorrow
That severs us.

My child rests
In eternal slumber
An empty void is my bequest
No more her frights
Can I allay.

She dwells forever
In sacred sepulchres of memory
In cathedrals of undying love
In the locket of my dreams,
And vast castles in the skies.

She dwells beyond
The hand of worldly misery,
Unsoiled by toil or cares
And to hold her close to me
Is beyond repair.

She romps, I am sure,
In a garden with love aglow,
Sheltered from earthly woes
Adorned in a mantle of peace
Hers forevermore.

My child sleeps, yes;
But in my heart she lives on
Watching with twinkling eyes over me
For now and evermore
My guardian angel.

The Lost Soul

A soul wandering in purgatory
Knows not where pathways lead,
Its anguish fills blue ethers
While struggles leave it beat.
The jungles of life behind it
Are revealed for all to see,
While the doorway so inviting
Hides what the future will be.

A moment was there for a choice,
But the second was lost in space;
That severed it from this race
Of angels who soar beyond it
To the paradise of reward,
But the soul now fights the battle
To pay for the mortal awards.

Oh, soul! Lost where winds blow,
Tossed by the traits that dared
To make life joyous at the cost
Of a danger without repair;
Go off into the dark hallways
Where fellow sinners wander
Amid the cries and the perils
Blocking you from heaven yonder.

Lonely are the eternities spent
With others as hapless as you,
Shamed in a society that molded
Evils shutting you from the blue;
Who knows what passes before

The thoughts that are a part
Of a soul now torn and tattered
Because once it lost its heart?

Recall, man, souls that wander
Devoid of love from anyone,
Which need prayers as stairways
To guide them towards the sun;
For if in life you understand
That death end not your life,
The Pilot at that gateway
Will steer you clear of strife.

Every Time
(An Elegy)

Every time someone I love dies,
   A little bit of me dies, too.
Every time someone I love hurts,
   A pain fills me, too.
Whenever a tear falls from a loved one's eye,
   I cry, too.
We are one in spirit and mind,
   What affects one affects the other.

Every time someone I love suffers,
   That suffering is mine, too.
Every time someone I love despairs,
   My world despairs, too.
Whenever there is the ache of loneliness,
   I am sad with longing, too.
We are as one in body and spirit,
   Parting cannot sever these.

Who can decry we were not as one,
   Or that our unity was complete?
Let us rejoice in our love that was
   And find solace in our loss
Until our paths shall merge afar
   And we shall be together again.

Book Two

Twentieth Century

Blind Is the World

Blind is the world to a soul
    sensitive in its search for good,
    reaching for knowledge of life,
    seeking serenity within the heart
    and finding naught but destitution.

Destitute of tranquillity
    is the soul which sees such evil
    as engulfs the pursuits of man
    who engineers schemes and ruses
    which leave mankind in anguish.

Anguished is the weary mind
    which cannot find much affection
    of man for his fellow or his friend,
    as both bicker over measly spoils
    that leave life twisted with torment.

Tormented are those kindly ones
    who seek to adjust man's flaws,
    who are buffeted hither and yon
    by despots who pettily berate
    them, leaving the world contrite.

Contrite are the peacemakers—
    insulted as moralists and crackpots,
    rebuffed by cruelties, which strip
    man of humaneness and dignity,
    thereby leaving them chastised.

Chastised are the fine hearts
    doomed to failure in endeavors
    that are aimed toward betterment
    of humans who will not listen
    to those of reasonable wisdom.

Wise are they who in their haste
    stop a moment, to soft words listen,
    gathering a morsel so appetizing
    which will nourish their spirit
    with greater serenity and love.

But love in this hasty world
    is a romance which few understand,
    accepting it as a feral emotion
    to be displayed in earthly spurts
    toward those who bring gifts.

And love is something great—
    finer than most hearts acknowledge;
    something that all life suffuses
    with understanding and tender peace
    and fills it with contentment.

But man destroys all love
    in his quest for power and lust,
    raping the world with his evil,
    plundering life of its joys
    and killing all hopes of eden.

Flight into Fancy

If I could but close my eyes
And find within the darkness
The bright light of my fancies
'Twould be a revelation—
For within this perfect refuge
Lies the virgin pasture
Sown with memories and dreams:
There is no bastion as sturdy
Nor river flowing as deep,
No star in heaven glitters
Bright as the star I keep;
What garden is more verdant?
Or where do trees grow as tall?
Nowhere is moonlight softer
Or winds fuller of murmured sleep;
Ah! if I could but close my eyes,
The miles would fall away,
And distance nothing would be
As I reach high for my dreams;
Too well I know something more:
Each dreamer is the richest,
My dream is the most beautiful
My thoughts ever the sweetest—
My blessing is the worthiest,
Where else match this perfection?
Who knows a downier softness
Or a more thrilling tranquillity?
If I could close my eyes,
How oft' hath these lips said,
If I could visit once again
This paradise of my dreams:

But life with all its bustle,
And inner greed for chattels,
Secludes the deepest desires
That in life a glen would create;
'Tis sorrowful I need admit,
For snared as others am I,
My heart yearns for paradise
While mind burns in hell's fire;
Someday I shall flee full haste
Into the ramparts of my dreams,
And clamber onto my shining star
Guarding that rich and quiet land.

The Treasure Trove

Twinkling lies crystal feldspar
'Neath shining stars above,
Sparkling gems of shimmering light
Delicate as the coo of doves;
Beautiful are summer rainbows
Across languid summer skies,
Fair to behold in fanciful flight
Accompanied by melody of sighs;
    The naked heart in red, red glory
    Beats out the wonders all about,
    The hidden soul in white purity
    Knows no refuge when love shouts;
    The wondrous elixir of daily life
    Is purified by each memory born,
    While the miracle of each hour
    Is stirred by the break of morn';
Sweet delight, sweet magic of night,
Songs of larks melodious, sweet,
The miracle of the sunset's glow,
Bask in marvels of nature's feats;
The roaring sea pelting white foam
With spray laving a tanned face,
The chill tingling down the spine,
All come and pass with little trace;
    Yet the gears of a spinning mind,
    Function and mesh in symphony
    To create the images that surfeit
    The beauty that minds ever seek;
    A cupboard of hours, evenly stacked,
    A priceless set of fragile Limoges,
    Guarded with a strong sentiment

And caring not whither time goes;
But the most treasured item fair
Resting on that shelf of time
Is that hidden from mortal view
And gazed upon with thrill sublime;
Covered with the dust of moments
Cleansed with feathery thought,
'Tis sparkling bright it glitters
As the article the mind sought;
　'Tis as though the searching eye
　Reached out and amid shining stars
　Selected the brightest that shone
　And the distance to it was not far;
　Or the dreamer on magic carpet
　Who glides to heaven in his sleep,
　There to wander in deep content
　Before the treasure at his feet;
　Wondrous indeed that many things
　Which spring up from unknown womb,
　Gaining beauty with each hour
　Are never laid in deathless tombs;
　Beautiful are these beauteous things
　But none more magnificent than this:
　Lovely beauty in the mind residing
　And which in sleep is ever missed.

A Tear and a Drop of Blood

Behold this fallen tear,
This drop of blood
From tired heart;
A tear? A drop of blood?
What play of words!
'Tis a mystic tale, alas—
For lost in wilderness
Of thoughts I wander
Whilst in the mire
Of hopeful dreams I seek
Escape from lonely hours;
A tear-stained old linen—
Wet a moment, then dry—
Leaving the remembrance
Etched in a vague splotch;
A drop of blood
Of life and not of veins,
Turning days crimson
With despair—and no hope;
Yet need I but move lips
In deep prayer and thus
Retreat into solitude;
Though I be there still,
Here I cannot be,
For off to dreamy lands
I run; my feet are rooted
To this ground, too true,
But my mind with celerity
Darts hither and yon,
Now aglow in autumn nights,
Then astir 'neath summer sky,

Here by a running brook,
Or there by a quiet lake;
A moment again in mountains,
Or an hour in a dim corner,
A tear to fall forever
To wash away the night,
A drop of blood whenever
Thoughts are in full flight;
Ah! My heart is cleansed
By a vague purity,
My eyes become sharpened
With visions of hope
That what was may ever be
The glory of this life;
I fear not otherwise
For the tear or drop of blood
Is mixed in distant realms
To fall on planted hopes
To bring prayers to bloom.

Without a Thought

In the quiet solitude of the woods,
  Beneath the spreading maple tree,
Man, perforce, should stop to think
  About the world in which he lives.
But what thoughts does he wander through?

If he were a bird up on that tree,
  And the whole world before him spread,
Would he fly away to a far off cloud,
  Away from the pestilence and mess?
What thoughts would in its mind spin?

If man were an ant scurrying to and fro,
  Traveling through the streets he made,
Witnessing misery of man's unkempt work,
  Would he flee to his ant colony
With a knowledge of man's utter futility?

The bird and the ant surely would see
  The ills and the evils of the world
Wrought by man's prejudice and stupidity
  Which leads to destruction of the soul
And the ruin of the intricate universe.

But the man who sits beneath that tree
  Is content to close his eyes and sleep,
Letting the troubles of the world go on,
  Until like the tree it withers and dies,
For to his problems man gave little thought.

Twentieth Century

Cast off the troubles and the toils,
For what good are they in life?
A jug of wine and dancing women
Are more rewarding than godly strife.
Music hath charm to soothe the soul,
So drink, be merry and be gay,
For darkness comes with sharp fangs
While the sun flees and none pray.
Open your heart to pleasures now,
Think not what the morrow brings,
Harken to the smoke-filled dens
And words debauched lips sing.
'Tis better now to live a life
To the full without design,
Lap up gems of touch and sense
Soon there may be no more time.
Laugh with clowns near or away,
Of life shape a trellis of mirth,
No reward remains when time ends
Save a hole in the meager earth.

The Brink of Doom

Once there was a purpose to life,
  Man sought to make a haven
Where he could live unmolested
  By the monsters of the world.
Predatory mammals were his foe
  And man to survive killed,
But his was a murder of necessity
  Not one of gluttony or hate.

But that seems changed forever,
  And through the years of yore
Man learned not to live in peace
  But became worse than ere before.
He learned to kill with science,
  Now the world lies at death's door;
He sought to enslave others' souls
  As he tracked mankind's spoor.

Alas, there seems to be no hope
  About to save man from despair,
He seeks not what God offers
  But the gifts soiled by Satan.
There is no peace upon this world
  And the brink of doom exists,
A dreary death life threatens
  Yet no one strives to resist.

Where is the love that bred us
  When life it first began?
Where are those joys of living
  In peace amid fellowman?

Must this bitterness continue
    Onto all earth's eternity?
Where will this ugliness lead us
    That fills hearts with such greed!

Cast off the search for pleasure,
    Seek not the worldly gains;
Reach not for gold and silver
    Or the spoils of deathly games.
These are short moments of life,
    Enjoy them while we may,
For life is just a very short fuse
    That God can snuff away.

It matters not what one may be,
    What counts is knowledge of love
Of man for man all o'er the world
    And especially for Him above.
Let devils roam in far-off hells
    Where they harm but themselves,
For us remains to make an eden
    Where naught but goodness dwells.

Science

The fading sun flees before the night,
Locking its shimmering hoard of gold,
And leaves behind naught save a glimmer
That on the morrow it shall rule again;
Now gently across night's nebulous seas
In gesture satin that soothes the sight,
A mellow moon voyages 'mid countless stars
To fill the void with its austere grace.
'Neath the alchemy lies a spinning world
In constant smoulder from human greed
Ravaged by frail souls mad with haste
To conquer the universe with atomic mace;
The world quivers as an orb enchained
From vapors sulphuric reeking the skies
That seep unfettered from magma brew
To choke and disfigure the earth's face.
    A man there was with ambition born,
    Who looked forward to the coming morn'.

Yon fiery spheres traversing the skies,
Dotting the blue as sequins on velvet,
Silently race aged orbits and paths
Across the vast tapestry of the night;
As sentinels hidden they preside and watch
Antics mad of scurrying creatures who strive
The universe to harness with puny might.
Which of the genii of the restive world
Can view guardians manning virgin skies,
Protecting the balance of power wrought
By justice adorned in aeolian right?
Who dares to trample on this worthy scheme

Which skypaths keep unencumbered and free
From dangerous diversions of mere man
That period a masterpiece sublime and bright?
   "The cosmos is a hapless thing;
   My plans will alter its everything!"

Beware lest judgment comes ere the dawn,
This world is still so frail and young,
'Tis ill the wind that breeds the scorn
In muddy minds of the droll mannequins;
Cry out instead to those guardians staunch,
Plead for their mercy that naught goes wrong,
Since wrath once stirred is a sharpened blade
Whose ruthless edge severs foolish things.
What fetid womb dared conceive the dreams
To cope with the delicate masterly plans
Existent from time immemorial and gone
And surviving 'til heaven earth's epitaph sings;
Alas! sorrow's pall dogs the earth's course
Nothing good springs from the hydra's head,
The lesson will be most difficult to heed
Once eternity's tocsin tolls and rings.
   Now helpless lies that ambitious man,
   Something went wrong with his meager plan.

Bitter Tears My Heart Shed

Cry, cry, my heart! Cry and cry,
Let fall tears as rain from black skies,
Flood the garden where there grow
The thorns shackling yon fair rose.
Shed a tear; shed a bitter tear or two,
Drown the harmful pangs so cruel
Which spring forth as wild weeds
Choking, choking a fruitful seed.

You knew fine beauty, still you tried
To harm it, nor asked you why,
And now you cry, oh, faithless heart!
So cry, cry! Beg for a new start.
These tears that fall make you so sad,
Yet a moment past you were so mad;
How could cruelty persist so long?
What devil nipped you with such wrong?

Now tears flow down burning cheeks,
As great sorrow within you reeks;
You blemished petals of a fair rose
With the fury of an anger's throes.
You dared crush it with rotting evil
Born of sadistic, tarnished devils;
Remorseful clouds darken the skies
Since the anger blinded your eyes.

Weary are you, oh, evil, evil heart,
Know you now where goodness starts?
Restore the fragrance that you tainted,
Return the bloom to the rose sainted,

Then sneak back to your nook obscure
Where your evil remains secured,
For your shame has weighed you down
With the thorns of a sinner's crown.

The Rulers—U.S.A.

I

Representatives of the people, you say?
By popular ballot were they invested.
And this licenses them to sit and rule
The people who cast their votes?
But did all the people vote for them?
Was it by unanimous consent?
I think it not, for there are those
Who dissented in the minority.
Majority rules is further argument
And those of lesser station must obey,
Still one cannot set the line too fine,
For he may soon be on the other side.

II

The Senator sits in the Senate seat
A master of his grandiose trust,
But he does not sit without bias
Since he calls himself of a party.
Republican or Democrat—should this matter?
Does not he represent all the people?
And this he should always remember.
To think otherwise breeds contempt;
Nor should the minority be overlooked,
For they live in the same country—U.S.A.—
Their taxes pay their representatives
And their flag is the same.

III

The Representative sits like a god,
   Thinking only of his job and votes,
For as soon as the investiture takes hold
   Politics become the rule of the game.
Party line and party bosses rule the hours,
   And the people at home be damned,
Except when to appease and soothe them,
   Otherwise the party line is the thing;
All else becomes of secondary nature
   Campaign promises fade into the past,
Only to be revived for fools to hear,
   Only to elicit again false hopes and cheers.

IV

And this corruptive ideal goes up and up,
   Until it touches all public servants,
Including Presidents who then look down
   Upon the voters and with deep frowns
Scornfully resent intrusion on their office
   While playing politics for party sake;
Republicans and Dems—Democrats and Reps,
   Smears and jeers, but always party lines,
While minority votes and majority too
   Look on amazed at the bewildering crew
Who are supposed to mould the laws
   By which all the citizenry must abide.

V

There was time of country first
Which the growth of the country nursed,
And whilst politics were dabbled in
The politicians listened to the echoes
Of voters who in great wrath could levy
Retribution upon lax office holders;
Now the public be damned and such
While taxation soars and business stifles,
While living has become a horrid thing,
So costly and without much hope
Of relief from the bureaucrats who ponder
How else citizens' money to squander.

VI

Sit ye rulers in your towers of ivory!
And frown upon those to whom you preach;
Gather in the wealth with greedy claws
While in the country welfare reeks
For those who need it and in despair seek
Alleviation from politicians' egos.
Oh, you care not for what voters say,
You cast aside all promises and praise
When midnight falls o'er election day
As you go merrily on your selfish way
To plunder hope and sow much sorrow
In hearts you lifted with your lies.

VII

The day must come for an accounting
   Of the manner of your stewardship
And how you did your citizens consider
   In the forming of the customs and laws;
Perhaps only then will you recollect
   That people are people and not pawns
To be pushed and shoved at your will
   While you squabbled in the party's grist;
Voters are but common ones who live
   In a country which brings much compromise
Of relief from cruelties of tyrants—
   But sometimes one must stop to wonder.

VIII

Tyrants make no pretense of their scheme,
   They usurp power and people slay,
Families are destroyed and riches burned,
   Bias stirred and emotions churned;
Wickedness can do naught but destroy,
   And all goodness soon does disappear;
But those gangsters too meet their doom
   At the hands of citizenry aroused;
Their great fault was lack of finesse—
   A choice ritual of the GOP and Dems,
But the end in both is always the same:
   Destructiveness and simmering hate.

Book Three

Of Derelicts and Diamonds

Of Derelicts and Diamonds

On cobbled street my footsteps passed
One January day; overhead the Third Avenue El
In the throes of its death rattles
After jostled decades of ingratitude and service
Clattered and clanked when trains roared by
As the avenue below trembled and quaked;
The rattling symphony pained the ear
While the din reached imperfect crescendo,
But the roaring sound soon hummed away
With but a whispering echo in the cold sky;
Bright sunlight filtered the aged lattice
Of wood and iron to cast truncated ghosts
On the street below where shadows played;
'Twas a strange sight on a cold winter day,
For the snow once fallen white now was gray,
And rivulets of slush rich with slime—
Which at night froze into speckled icy pools—
Splattered 'neath the frenzy of hasty footsteps
And whirring wheels. The Manhattan Bridge
In its solemn marble attire spewed vehicles
By scores and ten while the murky snows
Dulled the whine of the slipping tires;
Odd the paradoxes of man and life
As here amidst the clatter and noisy chatter
The ballet of life flitted on pirouetting toes
To bind the passing audience in blemished awe
At the deviationists and apostates
From spiritual and moral codes of society.
How weird the contrasting levels of man
Who frequented this confounded land
Like puppets activated by mystic strands

Guided and jerked by invisible hands!
What a miasma to behold and decry
For 'tis spoken well with reverent truth
That some had slashed constraining strings
And now travelled with unsuspended lust
Across the stygian wastes of a lost life.

Perchance, I walked along this territory
Of godless men worshiping bottled devils,
Clad in garments black from drunken sleep
On unwashed pavement or barren floors
Or charcoaled dirt by railroad tracks;
Unkempt, unshaven, decrepit in demeanor,
No ablutions here save of necessity,
No narrow roadway hedged with human codes
For these parasites. Nay, life was a gambit—
A survival from hour-to-hour; a struggle
To ward off the winter cold so bitterly
Surrounding them in outdoor abodes
With wind-whipped doorways as their beds
And old newspapers as blanket and sheet.
Lost dreams were valued wisps whose shadows
No longer fell on fertile hearts or minds;
Steady hands were strangers to habitués
Whose eyes were torpid from endless fatigue
From unquenchable fires of preying satans
That tormented their burnt-out stomachs;
Purple skin was leathery and cracked
From wind and sun. These were the bums
Who dwelled in skid row. These were the players
Unrealistic in their funny little worlds,
No longer dreamers of schemes and designs,
Nor with intrigue in this haphazard land
Except the skullduggery for a nip or two.

Long ago life had played out its hand
And in her tricks twisted these souls
To cast them on pernicious stream
Which flows into a sargasso sea located
In some jumbled realm. It was a blustery day
As the sunlight filtered through the tracks
On the slush and grime below. In the distance
The rumble of another train was heard
As the trestle again began to quiver,
But who paid heed? Not those who wandered
Aimlessly upon the dirty cobbled street.
How strange the environs of man!
Who will degenerate in a tangled morass
Worse than the existence of wild beasts
And who walk in misery and tattered frocks
Through the hours of a wastrel life,
Strangers to the wisdom of social gains
Or the depths of rich spiritual refrains;
At least this thought occurred to me.
Here in the wilds of thorny existence
Where poverty of heart and filth of soul
Ambled arm-in-arm, wealth the gamut ran
From nothing to plenty, from many to few,
From zenith to zero with tempestuous rage,
And the celerity of changing fortunes
In this iniquitous nest seemed odd indeed.
Such contrast! Such sharp machinations
Sickening to view and nauseous to behold;
Such contrast! Such weird manipulations
Of treasures in the name of business gains;
And yet which of these affluent souls
Who hastened passed the outstretched hands
Paused in reflection to take an account
Of himself—to tally the score of life,

There to sum up the value of living?
What philanthropist to survey the scene
Where man is scum, laden with the germs
Of failure to measure up to the challenge
Of life? What do-gooder scans this stage
O'er which walk these staggering actors
Dazed by the wounds of a poisoned life?

This train of speculation roared on me
As I watched on this cold January day,
And I wondered why armed battalions
Inspired with the contrivances of love
For fellowman could not march with might
Into scarred battlefield where devils
Carrying tridents of sour victory
Manned the ramparts against assaults.
Alas, this seems an enthusiasm vain,
For cohesion of attack impossible appears
When plans crash upon vague stratagems
Schemed by chiefs without warriors.
But there are rugged dedicated battlers
Who walk this fetid battleground of noise,
Who for many decades have forayed
Into this paved jungle, but whose attacks
Were foredoomed to dismal failure.
The heart shivers in the squalid splendor
Of this impenetrable forest of broken men
Which sprawls over a few city blocks.
Manhattan Bridge gapes out to Canal Street
Which to Holland Tunnel in turn leads;
Wheeled giants roar down its lusty incline
Across the cobbled street to distant places
Their bowels sated with the sustenance
And luxuries for a society more serene.

From night to dawn these monsters roar
And through the husky daylight hours too,
But care these denizens of the doorways
And sheltered corners? Nay! For the torpor
Of vain lives has conquered them
While the din is but the hazy invitation
Beckoning them where warmer clime rules;
Trains roar overhead and mad horns
Honk with the ferocity of enraged lions
Until the nerves grow weary and taut;
Farther south a few blocks more that bridge
So famous for the name it bears—that name
Symbolizing baseball diamond daffiness—
As vehicles spill from its fertile womb
In an unending steam. Contrast? Aye!
For broken men of broken ambitions
Who rot on sidewalks and in gutters
Clad in tatters and shod in broken leather,
Walk and stagger with red-rimmed eyes
Sunken in purple faces while limousines glide
To the curbs to discharge pompous gents
And buxom women in search of treasure:
Diamonds bright, rubies rare, emeralds fair.
In this garish hell a diamond center lies
Whose blue-lighted windows blind the eyes
With sparkling gems of color brilliant,
Intricate of cut and costly of price—
Jewels bespeaking of castles and kings,
Of pomp and circumstances, of gigolos and madams,
Of thieves and pawns, of intrigue and romance,
Of moonlit nights and beating hearts expectant
For emoluments to seal a promise or a prayer.
Intense the contrast for at the window bases
Here and there a drunken fool has gone

To visit the morphic realism of blankness,
And yet, perhaps, once he too had dreamed
Of jewels bright for a lady fair. Alas, alas,
What befell his hopes? Who can reveal it?
Dismayed was I to witness such as this
As footsteps slouched along sloppy snow
And eyes darted from bedecked windows
Agleam with the marvels of jewels bright
To dirty back tides of desperation which seem
To swarm over them to drown their lives.
Here Pell Street leads into Chinatown
Where gay lights shout from lanterns green
And fiery dragons and Chinese foods,
Where curio shops with mandarin clothes
And ivory elephants and statuettes of jade,
Where Chinese slippers and laughing Buddhas
Beckon the viewer to browse and buy;
This is the land where eager missionaries
Seek to gather together the stray wheat
Into a faithful bundle; where Chinese smells
Of Chinese food invite the gourmet's palate;
Here is the hodgepodge of Chatham Square
Dotted with hardware stops and cigar stores
And barber shops conducting "colleges"
For aspirants to the barbering trade
Who ply their inexperience on the derelicts
For a pittance in the name of practice—
These same shops who employ specialists
To deface the skin with obscene tattoos;
And here are Chinese markets with windows
Filled with jars of dried herbs and grasses,
Dried oysters, dried mussels, dried minnows,
Smoked hindquarters, smoked ducks, smoked all;
Here too on this avenue of dank despair

Are the clothing shops which specialize
In selling suits from four dollars and fifty
To ten dollars and usually a trifle more;
Surplus shops with decrepit surplus goods
Seek out the travellers of little fare,
What an Eden for ruthless entrepreneurs!
This kingdom of squalid creatures
Is rimmed with gadgets aged and modern
In juxtaposition to each other and yet
With eerie blending of the old and new;
On the corner of the Bowery and Canal Street,
Opposite the mouth of Manhattan Bridge,
One artery of the fluid diamond trade
Is crowned externally by a giant sign
Of neon lights and many red-faced clocks
Timing distant places across vast spaces;
'Tis a strange occultation filled with irony
For in the center is the New York time
While about elliptically shine the hours
Of the moment in London town and Paris,
In San Francisco and Sydney, Australia,
Not to mention distant Tokyo or Rome;
It is as though these storied places
Invited the vagrancy within the soul
Only to be drawn to a swirling vortex
Downtown in fabled land of skyscrapers;
Across the street is a palatial bank
Whose ruggedness snuggles it wealth,
Whilst on the roadway called the Bowery
Dealers of diamonds ply their trade;
Grand Street one block north is a festival
Of bridal shops standing in a row
Where white-laced mannequins live in windows
That glow, surrounded by ladies-in-waiting

Gay as rainbows, while at the slippered feet
Of these paper damsels of expectant dreams
Bridal books and lace from hiding peek.
Nearby lies Mulberry Street and Mott
With pizzerias and pushcarts selling wares
Of unimaginable sorts from pans and pots
To chestnuts and cabbage and prickly pears,
Men's shoes and hats; ladies' underwear
There are mission houses filled only
When police swoop down in sporadic raids
Averring to clean the streets and city
Of the motley crowds who it degrade,
Or the Salvation Army with its brave souls
Who work unstintingly to succor those
Who reach out despairing hands. Nor to forget
The dingy hotels with 50 cents per night rooms,
Or greasy restaurants with their specials,
Or the movie grist houses (who patronizes them?),
Or the plumbing establishments advertising
The most modern of modern conveniences,
Or the wholesale houses for restaurant utilities,
Or the antique shops with fantastic treasures
Of all descriptions—works of art and dreams
Which perhaps had once adorned carpeted rooms
With furniture to support well-fed humans,
Or the savings bank ubiquitous and huge
With its sparkling chandelier of light,
Or the electric shops with a million lamps
And ceilings dripping with crystals fair;
Perhaps the irony of this wondrous beauty
In antique shops frowning on broken men
Settled in the same amorphic land
Is too apparent for the naked eye to see
Since those once blessed with prominence

Were now levelled on the same thoroughfare
Both seeking in their peculiar mode
Salvation from their squalid environs.

Curiosity is a feline of hidden talents
Whose embrace is as silent as its stealth,
And whose influence leads slipping steps
Into the devious quarries filled with passion
For a more intimate and fruitful harvest;
Thus long after winter snows had melted
And summer heat had sizzled 'neath the El
I wandered aimlessly in this fairyland
Of derelicts and diamonds where brightness
And darkness clashed in violet depths;
The domain I roved was not unchanged
For autumn tartness and terse skies
Can paint a mural troublesome and stark;
Mulberry Street where oft' I traipsed
Was festooned in the glories of a feast
Framed in banners of red and white and green
(The Italian national colors, it seems),
And archways of lights stretched warmly
From Houston Street all the way to Bayard;
Refreshment stalls lined the narrowed street
On either side; an empty lot was decorated
With the Ferris wheel and other rides;
Store windows were gaily decorated too,
Emblazoned with signs and invitations new,
'Twas an event of greatest magnitude
Whose entrancement was open for all to view;
At night the hundred scores of lights
Glistened and sparkled like so many stars
Transforming the street into make-believe;
Humming throngs talking chit-chat,

Gouging themselves from stand-to-stand
With hero sandwiches of pepper and eggs
Or meatballs, or hot sausages, or salami,
Or munching on crisp slabs of pizza
Oozing with olive oil and tomatoes,
Sprinkled with mozzarella and oregano,
Or tasting roasted chestnuts hot from flames
Sending pungent scents into the night,
Or buying souvenirs telling of the feast;
Pushcarts stood between these many stalls
Bedecked with strands of roasted nuts,
And there were red pistachios and shelled almonds,
Mountains of pecans and toasted filberts,
There were dried figs and loose figs,
Walnuts and brazilian nuts—all kinds of nuts;
Peanut vendors plied their buttered wares
From mobile carts with whistles shrill;
There were fruits and many spices
From Italy or Spain. Snails for eating too
Were one man's ware nor was this quaint,
For the stores had deep baskets of this food;
The butcher shops exposed their meats,
Shanks of beef dangled in the windows,
Quartered rabbits fresh with blood
Were suspended in their furs for all to see,
Beef hearts and beef liver and calf brains
Reposed in shallow paper baskets
Red with blood were available to the view;
There were gaiety and laughter in the air,
Phonographs sent forth music loud,
People joked and people laughed—
For this was the lauded *festa di San Gennaro,*
Patron saint of the citizens of Mulberry Street;
Near Hester Street 'side an undertaker's shop

A large wooden altar loomed o'er the scene,
A tinselled giant of silver and gold—
Decked with myriad ribbons gently stirring
In the night air; the silver saint reposed
In its archive at whose broad base
Long streamers of silk dropped from the weight
Of dollars pinned in the expectations
Of indulgences from the intercession
Of a grateful saint; not far away
A bandstand dressed in colored muslin
Reverberated with cacophonic sound
From a skitterish band that had no fear
Of critics with poised pencil and pad
To write of merits of horn or woodwind;
The shuffle of feet hummed an accompaniment
Incessant in its muffled and brooding beat;
The buzzing voices so profound resounded
From the old adorned building walls.
The citizenry of the street lent local color
From festooned windows as they rested
On pillows laid across the windowsills
To gaze at milling crowds with patronizing smiles;
Loudspeakers cried out the inner thoughts
Of the eager cries exhorting the purchase
Of chances on the newest model Chevrolet;
Kerosene ranges in the stalls sizzled
And splattered with the hot olive oil
Frying peppers, frying sausages, frying onions
Whose sharp odors filled the stuffy air;
This was Mulberry Street in its hours of glory,
At its pinnacle of fame for the year;
This was the Mulberry Street of picture and song
Adorned in the gay dress of a fiesta
Which would leave the unbridled echoes

To haunt the street for the year to follow
Until the stands mushroomed once more
And shuffling feet and buzzing voices rang anew.

A vague mystic force propelled my steps
Until bewildered before that gilded altar
I stood face uplifted to San Gennaro,
And I watched the pious and the sinners
Come forward to utter cryptic beatitudes
Or pin dollars on the fluttering silken strands;
Thus intrigued I hardly felt the tug
Upon my sleeve and tolerantly I turned
Unknowing why such an act would occur;
There in crumpled hat and jacket torn,
With a week's growth of twisted black beard,
Stood one of those who tramped and begged
In that cobbled land not far away
From this gay mirth and raucous noise.
Perhaps my eyes were glazed by the sights
Of the feast, or perhaps my heart was opened
By the feted saint who looked benignly
Upon me from the shelter of his niche
High above my head. "Yes?" I uttered softly
As though the air were thickly sacrosanct.
Apologetically this bedraggled battered man
Replied with a strange and cultured voice:
"Can you spare me just a dime?"
This was a "touch" to myself, I whispered,
Hastening with mortal eagerness to answer no
When some strange power deemed otherwise.
"You know, sir," he said, "even bums pray."
Sacrilege! thought I in self-righteousness,
But then I wondered, *who am I to judge?*
Just another mortal who one unknown day

Could stand in the same fateful spot
Where this contrite man now stood
For judgment, and which of us was better?
Could I in truth reply it was me?
By the elbow of his filthy coat I took him,
Steering him through the joyful throngs
Until we entered a shadowy little park,
Sorely standing behind the Criminal Court,
On Bayard Street. And here in the gloom
Of air crackling with the festive sounds
We passed huddled forms in drunken sleep
Until an empty bench stared out of the night:
There, there, in our silence we sat down.
The September night whirred through the trees,
Lazy leaves floated to the black ground,
A funny chill passed through my spine.
I wonder, spoke I to my glum companion,
If a single question I could ask of him
And if he wanted to respond well and good,
Otherwise silent he could remain
And none the worse for doing so.
And in return I would see to it
That he would have his silver dime
And more too if he so wished.
A dime was all he wanted, he replied.
Well, we shall see. My heart beat fast.
His breath had the mustiness of muscatel,
An odor nauseous to the scent. I studied him:
His face was peaked and ashen with night,
While dark eyes tightly held the resignation
Of his fate. The beard was mottled with dirt,
Yet about his granite face there shone
An honesty of purpose and a truth of heart;
"Can you tell me why you spoke as you did?

That even bums pray? Indeed, for I have need
Of explanations. Pray tell me why."
"You look at me and see a bum. This is a truth
Which cannot be denied. But once upon a time
No tramp was I, but a dreamer with high hopes.
The foremost pinnacle of ambition was my goal,
To measure success with wealth at my command,
To rule an empire of steel and masonry
Together with all the people working inside;
I stomped on many hearts, crushed many souls
In wanton attempts to bless my hopes,
But instead I travelled a path to doom,
For I discovered wealth was a deep pit
Of emptiness swarming with insects and lice;
And difficult though the roadway to the top,
As easy, if not more so, the slide down,
And in my fall I became chained to despair,
A calamity of magnitude to sear the mind,
For when hope was gone, it burst into fragments
Wounding the heart and subjugating the soul."
Thus, in the eerie calm of September night
In deserted park save for disheartened dreamers
There unfolded before my heart and soul
The understanding of the truth that in all men
No matter what their circumstance
There beats an indelible spark of goodness,
A vision of faith, a divinity unexplained
By human words, but on tablet pure inscribed
In golden letters that kiss the stars,
My ears were attuned not to this sunken man
But to a phantom wraith standing near the sky
Which brought forth the puissance of hope,
Since hope was what he spoke of in a voice
Steeped by time in the malices of wine,

And each syllable and each delicate word
Was framed in the rich radiance of light;
Yea, long after I departed into the night
These roseate words recurred to allay my frights:

Hope is a seed within the mind,
A flower in the heart,
A prayer borne in the soul.
If you do not plant that seed, the flower
Will not flourish and the prayer is muted.
Hope is the soft whisper of a springtime breeze,
The rustle of the late autumn leaves,
The white purity of the new winter snow.
If you stifle the whisper and the rustle
Or 'smirch white snows, then hope is destroyed too.
Hope is the soft glow of the morning star,
The first twinkle of the evening star,
Or the sheen of full moons on placid lakes;
It is the refreshment of the aurora,
Or the delicacy of the painted dusk;
It is the kiss of a raindrop on thirsty earth
And the sparkle of dew caught by the sun.
Hope is an herb to salve the pains of life,
A wine to stun the mind of its flight,
A food to sate the hunger of the heart,
A medicine to resolve the uneasiness of being;
Hope is the threshold of salvation,
The flicker to dispel darkness of defeat,
The beacon to inspire one to ride out the storm,
The torch to lead the way for dreams to come true.
Hope is many things—
A wistful sonnet, a lover's dream,
The remembrance of a tender kiss,
A soft embrace, a caressing hand;

It is the lullaby of a mother to her child,
The regret of a meeting ended all too soon;
It is the dream of the future closely fondled,
It is the memory of moments nostalgic—
Aye, hope is many things.
Hope is the mirage of better things to come,
The yearning for life to bear its fruits;
It is the entrance into tranquillity,
The doorway to a peaceful garden,
The fragrance of a budding rose;
It is the bustle of the busy bee,
The scurrying of the anxious ants,
The contentment of a little calf,
The purr of a kitten, the cry of a crow,
The agitated bark of a dog for its master,
The whistle of a train far off in the night,
The glow of light to guide travellers in darkness,
The flutter of a flag rising in the dawn,
The emotion in the heart upon thoughts of home.
Hope is the seed and the flower of life,
The key to the doorway of ambition and desire,
Destroy hope and you destroy faith,
And without faith man is lost forever.

Oft' o'er the dark and dirty streets
My footsteps pass in new adventures,
But somehow there has been an alteration
Tho' these familiar haunts are the same—
A sordid impregnable jungle black with time
Inhabited by lost men of lost faith;
As I walk the ways of querulous mind
Or weave a path through staggering men
My eyes no more are clouded or befogged
By the righteous wall which a vain society

Has erected about me, for I have found
This is not a forest without salvation;
Unctuous preachers in constant endeavor
Strive to succor these miserable men
Who seem unwilling or unable to be saved.
Still the missionaries of all faiths
With the implements at their disposal
To shelter these unfortunate souls
From the malice sprung loose by society
Denotes a certain fierceful pride
That none shall fade into a morass
Without some helping hand offered kindly
To take the tottering soul and gently guide it
From that dismal land of bleakness
Into a garden where goodness abounds
And love of fellowman never perishes.
I need confess that oft' I pause
At that little hidden church on Baxter Street—
Precious Blood by the faith is it named—
There to pray in the somber solitude
Shattered only by the creaking floor
'Neath the footsteps of a visitor;
Before the votive lights, blue and red,
I kneel in a pew to shape words of weakness
Into a halting prayer of sorts
That the eternal grace of the rewarded
Who have achieved peace in distant heaven
Shall sow its strength of pure love
In all the barren hearts of those who pass
This iniquitous domain of fallen men.
The snow falls again on the old, old Bowery,
And winter brings anew the frigid garments;
The grime-covered buildings seem much dirtier
From the glare of the new-fallen virgin snow;

The ugly trestle is stark with the eeriness,
Icicles reach mutely for the street below,
Windows are covered with gray and blue frost,
The diamond marts sparkle with myriad light
Whose brilliance flashes in all directions
In gesture bold to seduce the pocketbook;
Gold trinkets, rubies and rich green emeralds
Rest comfortably on bewitching velvet;
The dingy bars seem dingier and more crowded,
The naked restaurants drone along as before,
The rumble of the train still sounds the same,
The quivering of the rickety trestle
Shivers and trembles on the street below;
Traffic from the bridges still spills out
Across the street hastening to leave the tawdry scene;
Pedestrians pause to look at jeweled displays,
Pedestrians hurry in all directions;
Mulberry Street and Chinatown are more dormant;
The bridal shoppes on Grand are more alluring;
The pawnshops and the plumbing houses,
The antique shops with their hoards of wealth,
The electric shops with a thousand chandeliers,
The cigar stores nestled in Chatham Square,
The Chinese shops with litchi nuts and jade,
The irresistible history of the environments
In halcyon days seem etched inexorably
Upon the static and strange mosaic of the present.
The snow falls gently, gently on the Bowery,
And the pedestrians' footsteps fade away
While crystal flakes whirl through the air;
Where are those denizens who on warmer days
Lay stupefied in gutters or doorways?
There are many hidden in slumlike crannies
Warmed by the hellish fires of cheap liquor,

Some wander aimlessly through the throng,
Shoulders hunched from the nipping cold;
Some are hibernating in distant unknown lands.
But the spring will come to the countryside
To bless it with fragrant buds and singing birds,
And as the hours of the day grow warmer,
As the snow and ice slowly vanish
Beaten bodies stir again in dark doorways
And tired feet tramp upon the dreary street.
The shops burst out in the splendor of yore,
That strange opulence of varied wares,
And sight-seers will walk in curiosity
Accompanied by the bark of hustling shills;
And life once more will be a veil of contrast—
Of brightness and darkness, success and failure;
Some former inhabitants of this forsaken land
No more shall walk the highway of life,
But for every fallen one a newcomer will rise
'Mid intonations of the pious saviours
And to the lethargy of the pedestrians.
Spring will come again and summer too,
And the Bowery of old will be the Bowery anew.

Book Four

Prisoners

Prisoners

I

We are prisoners of our dreams,
　　Victims of our hopes.
We are captives of our desires,
　　Slaves of our habits.
　　　　We are not free!

II

We are prey to our prejudices,
　　Shackled by our bias.
We are wards of our fears,
　　Guardians of our imagination.
　　　　We are not free!

III

We are cloaked by our heritage,
　　Stripped by our greed.
We are blinded by our anger,
　　Maimed by our jealousies.
　　　　We are not free!

IV

Freedom lies in charity and love
Urged by a caring heart.
Freedom rises from an open mind
Willing to do good deeds.
Dare we to be free?

Reflect a Moment

If importance, lust or rancor
    Fill your heart as buzzing bees,
Stop, reflect a moment,
    Be more of what you should be.

If you're growing greedy,
    And avarice is nigh,
Take a look into a mirror
    Be little less of what you are.

If you think the world's against you
    And things seem to go awry,
Be more of what you should be,
    A little less of what you are.

When the whole world seems appalling,
    And you're steeped in misery,
Be less of what you are,
    A little more of what you should be.

Alone one cannot wander,
    Alone one cannot stand;
Be a servant to all mankind,
    Stretch out your helping hand.

The Beggar

If in this life I were a beggar,
    Content to beg upon the street,
What would I ask the people for?
    What wealth would I entreat?

Perhaps I'd ask for gold and such
    Or a trinket made of silver,
Maybe it'd be something unwanted,
    A fragment or a splinter.

What I received would be in thanks,
    For it would do me good,
But all these things do not me please
    As much as something else would.

For though I begged with open hands,
    'Twould not be with my heart,
And what my voice to people ask
    Of me would not be part.

Other thoughts of begging mine would be,
    Something that wealth can't buy,
It would have to do with a dream
    That'll haunt me 'til I die.

I'd beg for just a little smile,
    And a glance that comes from you;
A tender word and a thought of two,
    Would make my dream come true.

This then would make me rich and big
    And though I'd starve or thirst,
My heart would be ever on fair you,
    All else would be but worst.

And when all else would quiet down,
    And streets deserted be,
These riches with me would I take,
    These that remind me of thee.

The Best of Friends

Seek you the richness that grows
Within the heart like a lily pure?
Sending a fragrance to the mind
Overcoming all bitterness and rows;
Reach for the wonder of the soul
Stretching before thee as the sea,
Powerful and mighty with each sigh
That steers you towards a golden goal;
Touch the beauty of your thoughts
Which unveil themselves as the sun
To dispel darkness of the dawn
And banish fears the mind has fraught.

About are all the food one asks
To satiate hunger of the soul,
Until it fills and softly reclines
'Neath a new tenderness relaxed;
Hunger not for matters too real,
Thirst not for frailties of man,
Console yourself with ideals strong
Which ever to idle moments appeal;
Then will you understand this verse,
That infinite are the unknown things
Protecting thee from morn 'til night
And guarding you from evil's curse.

What do you need to give thee this?
Be not limited in your human scope;
Dig deep about you, life has hope
That shall uncover a hidden bliss;
And you shall harvest a mighty feast

Opulent enow for the mightiest king;
But pray not to fall into evil ways
That will burden you as a beast.
In innocence was mother's child born,
Then it grew 'mid man-made thistles,
Threatened it was with weeds and burrs
From the sunrise of life's dawn.

And through the days place yourself
With people and things that bring
In themselves knowledge of the good
That more in them you wish to delve;
Then only will you find such delight
Brings power to contend with the earth
And whose force soon is neutralized
As you travel easier on your way;
Remember then these admonishments:
Give much, seek naught in return;
Toil with patience, loll with ease,
These shall make thee best of friends.

A Quartet Who Live?

The rich man counts his wealth in gold,
The poor man counts his dreams,
The politician looks around for votes
While the robber schemes and schemes.

I wonder which of all these men
Is content with life on earth,
It seems to me that in the end
They will all end up in dirt.

And when that fateful day befalls
The rich man with his wealth,
Were all his efforts and his toil
Worth depredations on his health?

The poor man too one day will die
And his dreams crumble to dust,
Will those hopes which he conspired
Remove the fair casket's rust?

The politician seems the worst of all,
For his crimes are against all men,
He robs the people with his talk
While burning candles at both ends.

The robber schemed and got nowhere,
His loot did not bring peace,
And when he leaves for fires of hell,
Will his schemes and looting cease?

The world is full of various thieves
Who wallow in loot and lust,
But poor man, rich one, or the sneak
All will turn into gristle and dust.

The rich man robs himself of life
As night circuits he survives,
He lives amid turmoil and strife
With little purpose to his life.

The poor man wastes his precious time
With ambitions he seldom shows,
All his dreams seem worse than crime
As in life he squanderly goes.

None are as bad as that politician,
Even Satan will rant and rave:
"Let not enter this mad magician
Or my soul he'll try to save!"

The thief and conscience are at odds,
His crimes are cunning and cruel,
But if he thinks retribution escapes,
Then he is a vain and stupid fool.

The moral is to live a life
Without a single sin,
But if such a man there ever lived
Then I'll get drunk on gin!

The Fugitive

A fugitive from smile-covered lanes
Is a lonesome wanderer indeed,
Floundering in fetid pools deep
With stagnant weeds of worry;
Quivering with the chill of sorrow
Whose icy tentacles of concern
Rack the mind, the fleeing heart
Roams lost in forests of perdition.

Behold this captive of blackness
Enveloped by the stifling folds
Now exhausting the lightened soul
That once glittered in mantle white;
Doorways to memories are covered
By brambles of confusion and fear
That stand with thorny spears
As guardians against happiness.

Oh, to tear down the poisoned vines
Entwined about the baneful soul,
Choking off the stream of joy
That now meanders in a far-off bed;
Hand up the ax shaped of laughter
To hack away the black roots,
For thus will die the evil vines
And unveil the doorways anew.

Short time it takes, though a second
For the thorns to bare their edge,
And once armed the foes of joy
Cannot be easily annihilated or destroyed

But persistence against darkness,
Will penetrate misery's armor
Which disintegrates and limply flees
Into the stygian swamps and fens.

Give this wanderer a weapon—
HOPE—and soon will be surmounted
The obstacles barring the return
Onto the footways of contentment;
So despair not all you of prayer,
The weapon waxes staunch in hands
That hack away at poisoned roots,
Which blot contentment from the mind.

The Mind's Refuge

The winter winds howling fierce and strong
    With chilly blast knifing gray air,
Sending tremors through barren trees,
    Chasing clouds 'cross murky skies
While billowing snow swirled and danced,
    White-hooded dervishes frenzied and mad,
To wailing tunes cleaving eerie air
    Piling whiteness into shadowy gloom.

No laughter echoes and all was still,
    Faces peered through curtains drawn
With startled eyes and mind turmoiled
    While aching pangs stabbed at the heart
As snow drove against windows frosted,
    Roadways cluttered with fearful throng,
Footsteps hastened to fireside's warmth,
    Heads bowed and collars tightly drawn.

        Blow on, ye winds! Blow with thy might!
        Before thee lies the cowering earth
        Frozen by thy talons iced and chilling,
        Blanketed by white of snow a-stinging
        Storm on, ye messengers of the north,
        Sweeping into hiding all in thy path,
        Closing the doorway of the summer past
        Secluding hours in a blanket white.

Yet by thee love is ne'er overcome,
    Secure in knowledge storms must expire,
Returning the mind to hours aglow
    When thy breath lies stilled in arctic snow;

And though ye rage, friendlier days survive,
　　Flashing onward as a mental torch
Whose blessed warmth thy cold rage endures,
　　Bringing faithful worship to my heart.

Gardens of the past in fragrance bloom
　　With an incense that captivates this night,
Warding off the chill howling so strong,
　　Filling cold hours with love ever bright
That from my windows in anger winds turn
　　To flee through the night to a lengthy sojourn
Embittered that though all bows 'fore its might,
　　One soul exists its cold to fight.

　　　Blow on, ye winds! Blow with thy might!
　　　Somewhere blooms a flower in glory sweet
　　　Unscathed by all that thou may exert
　　　Upon a delicate beauty never conquered;
　　　Storm on, ye messengers of the north,
　　　This flower from thee shall never flee;
　　　Nay! It shall tower through darkened hours
　　　To bring back summer's loving memories.

The Mood

Once I ambled with gay leisure
Through the primrose path
Where sunlight gilded the trees
For gay sprites who sat
Upon mossy banks with vivid eyes
Watching my foolish antics,
As I traipsed and danced sublimely
On the banks of the River Eros.

My heart was a vessel of roses
Suckled by petals that fell
With each throb, and my soul
In aphrodisia and song was whelped;
Footsteps bristled on red coals
Of desire that flamed and flashed
Until I was foot-weary and tired
By foolish antics of my soul.

Oh, desirous are the blossoms
Plucked by the devilish Puck
Who aims an arrow straight at me
As on your wonders I dwelt.
The vintage is old but antics
Are as young as a newborn babe
Who finds novelty in everything.

The satin moon shimmers o'er the
Green field while stars cast
Shining light upon the heart so
Romantic with a love hidden from
Sight; but the moon in all its glory

Knows the miracle pure and chaste
Laving the mind of man's wicked
Plans that life wastes.

Now I stagger in woods of despair
Where the flowers used to grow,
Where petals are choked by brambles
Pricked by the thorns of the dead rose
Of weariness and the rambling soul;
The path is steep and precipitous,
Boulders are strewn in my way
The gay sprites have disappeared
From mossy banks where they sat.

The River Eros is in a torrent
And the skies overhead are black,
The bower of roses is wilted
From a love that does not come back;
The incense is all scattered
By winds puffed with evil designs,
While the red coals are the ashes
Smoldering in Puck's sighs.

The Nomad and the Mariner

The nomad lost in desert wastes
Beneath the broiling sun
Is blinded by white heat and endless sand
Stretching farther than he can see,
And he staggers with thirst,
Weary of body and fatigued of mind,
Ready to give up the unequal struggle
To lay his head upon the hot sands in
      eternal sleep.

The mariner tossed on boiling seas
Where wild winds and waters howl
Is sprayed and lashed by whipping foam
Thundering across the plunging bow,
Weary of body and fatigued of mind,
Ready to give up the unequal struggle,
To lay his head upon the wet deck in
      eternal sleep.

But wait! Look yonder! Is that water
To sate the thirst, to refresh the body?
Is that the sun to quiet the seas,
To warm the body and bring fresh hope?

One wants what the other does not,
Death to one is salvation to another;
A drop of water to soothe the heat,
A ray of sunshine to dispel the cold;
But if the positions were reversed,
Would that which had been sought
Still be the motivation and means
To raise one from dark despair?

It is all in the circumstance
Wherein one finds himself;
Hope, faith, despair are but one
Crucible of dross and bubbling metal—
And the dross must be ladled off
Until clear boils the shining pool,
That one becomes a wiser man
Where before he had been a fool.

Some seek the darkness, a black veil,
To hide from all that is contrite,
But for everyone in this position,
There is one who seeks the light.

The nomad will find his water
With which to slake his thirst;
The mariner will discover the sun
Which shall quiet the plunging bow;
Oh, somewhere in the lost horizon
Are the secrets we never can know,
Yet destiny will shape the conditions
To follow our steps where they roam.

Despair today; tomorrow a ray of hope;
A drop of water to soothe the heat,
A ray of sunshine to dispel the cold;
These will come if these we seek,
For 'tis wiser to live in concert
With a plan unknown to us
Than to struggle in the dank corners
To formulate schemes of our own.

The Storm

The waters of the sea, rolling, rolling
From the horizon whence they rise,
Thunder, shout, and pound the beach,
Resolutely plunging onward,
Shrilly ebbing through the reeds,
Pushing pebbles on and on,
To fill the air with wet sound.
   Barefoot stands the boy before this might,
   Trickling water boiling at his feet,
   Head turned towards the flying spray,
   Scanning rollers tumbling on their way.
Breakers coiling, breakers falling
From the crest whence they rise,
Buffet angrily the breakwater
Scorning mortar and concrete,
Racing towards a futile end,
Breaking fiercely on and on,
To retreat limply on the swell.
   Barehead mariner strapped on the prow,
   Washed by the spray lashing round,
   Thoughts attuned to a warmer clime
   With dancing wavelets more sublime.
Gray clouds before the gale streaking
From the chaos whence they rise,
Race across the morbid seas,
Tormenting waters into a rage,
Revelling in frothing waves,
Speed towards the cottaged bluff.
   By the lantern stands she waiting,
   Mind concerned and lips that pray,
   Listening to the waves that crash,

Unmindful of the ocean's spray.
The ocean's anger subsides swiftly,
Gone the fury to whence it rose,
Serene lies the rolling sea,
Softly lap the quiet waves,
Breezes sing across the dunes,
Through the reeds playing a tune,
As clouds fill the air in dusky calm.
Barefoot boy returned to the cottage,
Praying woman from the window turned,
Mariner unleashed from the mast,
All is quiet—the storm has passed.

The Yearning Heart

Give me the wind that blows through my hair
    And the smell of the ocean breeze;
Let me join the chorus of singing birds
    Who fly unchallenged and free.
Let me float through space on fleecy clouds
    To survey the world below,
And bathe my heart with the light of the stars
    As through this world I go.

Let me ride with the moon in nocturnal flight
    Through heavens soft and blue;
May I be laved by fresh snow on the hills
    With a cleanliness sweet and true.
May my soul wander through flowered fields,
    Overcome by the scents so sweet,
Where I become aware of a fragrance
    Which makes life more complete.

Let me face the sun at the break of dawn,
    When darkness flees so fast;
Let me live in the joy of breaking morn
    In that peace that rarely lasts.
Would that across the earth I wandered
    To a haven hidden and pure,
Where I would find the peace I seek
    For all life's evils to cure.

And at night when the moon so afire
    Rules the enormity of space,
Would that I lay in fresh-mown hay
    Away from a world so crazed.

So let me look to the heavens high and far,
  To that home for which I long
Amid the creatures unchained by this life
  Where plans may never go wrong.

A Weed or a Flower

On stern foreboding crags of life
Plundered and scaled by ires and mores,
As daggers keen to pierce bleeding flesh,
Man scans horizons for vague perfections
Of time and things in nebulae concealed
While glazed eyes gaze ever backwards
O'er slouched curve of ladened shoulder
At the creaking gate of a dying past
Slowly closing to the point of no return;
Man searches for the petulant prints etched
On mossy banks of a virile youth,
Streaming through glades of happiness
There to list' to the gurgling echoes
Of a peace carried only by the young;
But all seems fogged in glens of memory
As the lane of life sprawls and turns
With length unknown and gradient hidden,
O'er which lurk obstacles conspiring;
None can tarry in the fickle present
Never confined in sleek slippery robe
Misty to the touch, musty to the smell;
Man grasps the sensuality of today,
Striving to contain it, alas! To no avail,
For time is such a temperamental lass
In mystic veil wielding a ponderous hand.
Resolute the traveler, staunch or weak,
But owner not of strength to stem the tide
Which sweeps upon him as debris on surging seas,
Seeking to trip his scurrying heels
One step ahead but inexorably slipping
'Til the fateful cutthroat day arrives

And footsteps falter and hapless the one
To retard the inundation closing o'er him
That no more to talk in life, dead he lies.

Sow a seed where a flower will rise
From fertile soil which in its time
Shall scent the air with fragrance fair
To fulfill plans of a hand benign;
The blossoms will bloom in perfect hue
To gild the scene, and its intimate being
The earth enriches, if but for a moment,
The better for having bred that seed.

Mark ye time a moment if you can,
And to these words lend an errant ear
That ye may pause in deep reflection
To piece the ragged puzzle called life;
But more, are ye as the sweet flower
The better for having been, or just a weed
Choking goodness striving to emerge
To sprinkle the air with a chaste scent?
The bee in flight gathers pollen sweet
To carry it away, yet in its busy toils
Pauses to dust beauty on other plants,
Bestowing thereon an intimate embrace
That on earth will flower a mantle gay
To luminate days that might dawn gray,
And fill some hours with the delight
Of blessings to enrich life's flight.

Are ye a weed, I must ask.
Or a flower 'side which to bask?

Our Trail to Eternity

You say to me this is not so,
This is something not to be,
Yet if you gaze about you
There is much for eyes to see.
Who knows what God has meant
For those whom He creates?
The golden portals are ajar
For those whom He awaits.
Meanwhile let us forge ahead
In life with clear calm thoughts
And seek the best happiness
That hearts have ever sought.

Questions rise swiftly and quick.
One asks what plan is this?
Who are we to comprehend?
What fills our lives with bliss?
The stars were made forever
To recline in velvet skies,
While my pulsating heart
Was made to beat at your side;
My soul is filled with nectar
When your beauty comes to view,
If my heart I give to you,
May yours return this love true?

The wayfarer never pauses
To question what he notes,
Nor do artists stop to weigh
Hours of art they may devote;
The sailor sails the seven seas

With face turned to the wind,
Though storms his ship may turn,
He knows he has not sinned;
Likewise must we continue
In our journey through this life,
Aware only of the happiness
And avoiding the snares of vice.

If this then will be our aim,
Surely a goodness follows,
Joy will be our daily bread
With moments blessed and hallow;
Turn your wisdom to the sun,
To the glow where pureness shines,
There shall we see the treasures
To make our lives sublime;
So let your heart be naked,
That its beauty I may see,
If thus our souls we do blend
We shall capture eternity!

Book Five

Love

The Searcher

I wander in the wastelands
Of thirst for one more kiss,
And roam the hoary mountains
For a glimpse of my young miss.

And when the moon ascends
The heavens in all its glory,
The winds will hum the lullaby
Of a lover's sweetest story.

Love

I

Love immortal burns as mystically as velvet hues
Of night to warm a vacuum questing its kiss
While the silver sequins adorning the skies—
As many sparkling diamonds radiant and pure—
Shower flashing sparks upon love's sweet bouquet,
And the watchful flames of powerful Thor
Are limitless, nor constrained by fleeing time,
While Pan dances with golden pipes upon a heart
Submerged in the Styx of life's tumbling rapids;
Musician pert, soothe this spirit with your notes,
Cast me adrift 'neath peasant sun and poet's moon
Where I may lounge in your symphony.
Place me in yon crucible molten with passion's fires
Where aesthetic wonders bubble in woven bowers
Of ecstasy and flames of adoration unsullied
While sibyls blend seraphic voices in a choir
Extolling the virtues of tender hearts afire
With the toxic elixir of Venus and Adonis
That wafts incense which all peril endures.

II

Love! What tranquil magic! Oh, petulant fruit,
Stirring life with the power of snowcapped hills
Crowned by the amber light of a regal sun!
While purity hath the womb of sweet inspiration
Recoiling from the whiplash of farinaceous touch;

Eros with eager lips of gold list' to a plea,
Hearken to the prayer that from a captive heart flees.
Oh, adoration more effusive than moonstones
Bewitching eyes cast to an evil sorcerer's brew:
Oh, endless passion opulent with giddy memories
Enchanting the eve' while seconds drip away;
Oh, glorious strength more dormant than seas at calm,
More austere than nebulous whiteness piled high;
Love! Dissipating winds choking black shrouds
That strive to extinguish the fires you bring;
Oh, eternal serenity; oh, glowing and graceful heart!
Speed swiftly into this barren and wasted domicile;
Carry your delights with compassionate torch,
Which will guide me into your paradise so rich.

III

Love exquisite aspired to by man through ages,
Flits from hour-to-hour and heart-to-heart
With the swiftness of Diana keen in her hunt
Unfrocks the shadows with her silver shafts
That life may blossom into a garden of dreams.
Rare comfort returns with your merciful charm,
Powder me with stardust; bathe me in summer's breeze
Poured for moments when joyous lovers meet.
Much solemn emptiness is born when longing arms
Are shorn of their love, and time gnaws drearily
Until forlorn pangs of hunger fill the heart;
Chaste Agape with thy goodness, lull this mind
With a delicate kiss, lip cast upon ruby lip,
And in your arms enfold me with a warm embrace
Which will dispel the gnashing ills of night;
Mount the thrill of her presence, the closeness

Of the infinite wonders pressed to my breast;
Love, love! You know these secrets bold and well,
Dare I repeat them ever, pray to tell!

IV

Angels come but never depart and so does love
That glides on starlit beams from paradise—
A white cloud of innocence crowning a lamb
Who wanders recklessly across highways of life
From the second when the muses brushed his heart.
Sensuous nectar stirred by the fragrant throbs
In hearts benumbed as though by Bacchus's breath.
Yonder emerge new vistas, basely unexplored
Into which the insensate lovers stumble unafraid,
Discovering the hidden treasures once veiled
From sight, but now the pallid heart is clement
In its new adventure guided by a sturdy soul.
Intrepid explorers unmask darkness, and marvels pure
Bloom vividly when Diana loosed her glow
Exposing garlands of delight in biased flares.
Oh, lover, resting in the pastures of your mind,
Surrounded by a shining love so chaste and kind,
In your fitless slumber travel into the court
Of the kingdom where this fruit of love was sown.

V

Oh, beauteous love, sweet morsel for heart and soul!
You bring new sustenance surging through veins,
Swiftly coursing into splendid plans and dreams
As lovers reside in the silence of unspoken words

Revealing emotions from which castles are built.
Your glorious burst of light exiles the gloom
To stygian depths no more it comes forth:
Love's tacit thoughts of significant intent
Birth wisps of moonglow in your heart,
Crowning lullabies e'en as time is stilled.
Oh, words of comfort! Oh, speech of gracious wisdom!
Oh, confidence nurtured in love-struck sky!
Your brilliance pales the flames of brightest gems
And subdues the fires of muted stars.
All treasures are lost in the disuse of poverty,
Outmatched by the precious wealth of silent love.
Lovers seek their finite richness without wit,
Cascaded into a garden aglow with incense
That sprinkles heaven's light into their souls,
Filling them with power time cannot shatter
Nor life with its heavy tread expend.

Love: A Stream and a Mountain

Behold yon mountain bold
Silhouetted against the sky,
Towering high, tall and strong—
An implacable fortress
Verdant in spring,
Brown in summer,
White in winter,
Russet in fall;
Behold yon mountain staunch
From whence this stream flows,
Gurgling coldly and swift,
Refreshing the course it runs—
Frozen in winter,
Thawing in spring,
Sluggish in summer
Vibrant in the fall.
Likened to the mount' is life:
Varied temper 'neath the sky,
Oft' impenetrable, oft' gray,
A chimera on some days;
A mountain and life,
One endures and one flees,
A stream and love,
Both flow pleasantly;
Yet love is a mountain
And life is a stream,
The former are lasting
Whilst the others pass on;
Tempests in yonder hills
Are different than love?
Lovely yon mountains,

More lovely than love?
Love like the stream
Passes to varied realms
Yet always resurging
From the source of its birth;
Love like the stream
And love like the mountain,
Cool and white,
Frozen and thawing,
Vibrant and sluggish,
Refreshing and verdant;
Different? Nay!
Confusing? Ay!
But in the confusion
Is the loveliness of love.

Love's Glory

Today you walk as of the past,
Tomorrow the dawn breaks anew,
Yet life forever will be altered
As it freshens with a sweeter dew;
Graced will be your life, I say,
With contentment and full bliss,
And blessed with a godly splendor
Of the magic of a morning kiss;
The sun will rise o'er your lives
Amber goodness will shine bright,
May all the wonders of this day
Through all hours be your light;
Contented and with new courage
Enter your Valhalla of sweet joy
Let overflow the cup of happiness
That with majesty mantles all.

So when the dawn breaks new
May your plans as starlight glow,
From the silver tree of magic
In the glen where contentment grows;
Your pathway lies before you.
This event by heaven was planned
As we upon earth are guided
By a loving and gentle hand;
Let your heart in tender smiles
Reveal all that you hold near
For in each other's presence
Will blossom life precious and dear;
And in all your quiet hours,
Will the memories in sweet ascent

Fill the garden of your love
With a fragrance never spent.

What Would I Give Thee?

What would I give thee above all else?
   This heart so pitiful and base suggests
A gift unseen by struggling defiled man
   Who is governed by weird abusive plans.
I beg this mind alien to fine sense:
   Canst though reveal the gift for one so fair
That the world might come to understand
   The tender strength of her guiding hand.

Speak out, cry out, from mountains shout,
   To this universe do proudly proclaim
The message burning fiercely in this heart
   With a searing pain that cannot be forgot.
Yet tenderly beseech the vast angelic host
   To echo these words with golden throats,
That forth may resound music sensuously,
   Echoing softly its peal melodiously.

Come, come! you have dallied too long;
   A moment more and you may lose this song,
So while the lyrics burn high and plainly
   Emboss them with flares for all to see.
Delay not the message aflame in this soul,
   Repressions belong to the hapless ghouls;
Recall precious words so often said
   In a mind where sad tears are bred.

What would I give thee? Need you ask?
   The whole world may take me to task
For utterances so seemingly bold
   Or dreams that my heart strongly holds.

Still someday this world that now scorns
    This mind may see a miracle reborn,
Where resides a beauty for all to see,
    A celestial image belonging to me.

I give thee a heart so humble and poor
    And a mind smitten by your kind care.
These lips do offer you sweet words,
    Gathered in a mind fertile with seeds,
Planted by the hours that were shared
    'Neath the intimate glory of your grace.

The seedlings bloom into idealic spirits
    Who stride in gold-threaded slippers,
Carrying lanterns that shed starlight
    To consecrate the vivid tho' slumbering past.
And I add the incense within my veins—
    Those delicate emotions lying prostrate
Before the glorious captor who enraptures
    A soul that revels in its welcomed capture.

To this fate my heart never rebels,
    Those hours you gave remain citadels
Against attacks upon dreams so sweet,
    Which tower sternly to soothe my needs.
I give thee my heart with trembling hands
    Upon which, etched as on time's sands,
Are messages as priceless as the stars
    Chastened by your loveliness so far.

What would I give thee? Is there more?
    Ah! The world can never know such wealth
Garnered by a nomad mind enriched
    By the treasures past hours wrought.

I give thee the praises of this earth
   To paint the beneficence of your caress,
I shall frame it in the rainbow's curve
   For all to see the angelic masterpiece.

Pockets are unlined and the purse is lean,
   Silver tinkles not and lack of gold have I,
But wealthier than I lives not a man,
   Either now or from when life first began.
Pauper though I be, this gold I give thee,
   This love surpassing all else on earth,
Shining forth in a halo of sparkling gems,
   So matchless in purity and depth divine.

The kneeprints pressed where humbly I beg
   For a longing gaze upon your beauty clean
Is the greatest treasure I would pay
   Until life enters its last fateful days
For beggar am I, bold enough to supplicate
   'Neath the warmth your smile radiates.

What would I give thee? Again you ask?
   My weary mind and soul so fatigued,
That you might revive them with a kiss
   From the soothing sanctity of your lips.
More, I present all my knowledge so bare
   That you may take and inspire it to heights
From which I shall cry for all to hear:
   You are the one who made life so dear.

What would I give thee? Life should know!
   There must a clarion call to the sky
Where the stars shall cast a mellow light
   Upon these thoughts poured into the night.

I give thee a kiss 'neath the summer's moon,
Tender love words to dispel the dusk,
And songs of birds high in graceful flight
Echoing daintily through velvety nights.

I give thee trees draped in autumnal hues,
Guarding a placid lake under skies of blue,
Where enveloped by wealth of joyful hearts
We came together never more to part.

I give thee raindrops that musically fall
In a pleasant park circled by trees so tall
That seem to weave a spell of magic
In a world so morbid, so mad, so tragic.
I give thee dreams without remorse,
Branded in a mind, fired by their source;
And no need exists to count this treasure,
I present it to you with heartfelt pleasure;
May it be the guidepost in our lives
Leading to heavenly, eternal paradise.

All these I give thee until time departs
Into the darkness where all humans debark
From which there is no return to this earth,
No beauty of minds nor children's mirth;
Take these I offer and hold them close
That their costliness to all will boast
Of this humble heart wherein was etched
The brilliance of a love that never wept.

And when in silence you live with thoughts,
Remember the glory which to me you brought,
For this mind can never retrain its soul
Which flees to your haven in manner bold.

Take up this pulse that throbs rich and soft,
  Hold the warmth of tender embraces aloft;
Reach through the years for memories sweet
  When for short seconds our lives were complete.

With all strength within I strive to present
  A wholesome love to make your life content,
That in solitude will grow recollections
  About the love you wove to such perfection.
This then I give thee swaddled in the gold
  Of a loving heart and an enraptured soul.

The hours are long and slowly do tread
  Into the gloomy corners of the past,
Where they gather stardust until recalled
  In silver garments cleansed and scoured.
This is the fate levied upon all hours,
  They are pressed like lovers' flowers
With nostalgia, between pages of a book
  Which is hidden in a secretive nook.

These I Give Thee

I can give thee naught but love
That thunders and breaks with might
Upon the crystal shores of our lives
Where we stand bathed by the stars;
My wealth is this within a heart
Aflame with the luster of gold,
Yet costlier than earth's metals
Is this fire beyond the eye.

I give thee a purity which grows
Within a soul bare of evil's claw,
Which adores thy priceless beauty
With piety reaped from paradise;
For thou can only be idolized
By perfection of heart and soul
Strangers to sordid thoughts and ways
That despoil beauty heaven-sent.

I give thee but a soulful glance
Drawn deep from a sacred well
From which drink lovers in quest
Of love crowned with halo bright;
Naked does my soul present itself
That thou may comprehend this truth
Swaddled in white of infinite grace
Because thou descended from Eden's race.

Oh! This gaze turned upon thee
Is filled with chastity of thought,
While this mind in cleanliness roams
Through snow-white beauty thine own;

Not for a solitary moment can I
Succumb to temptations of body or mind,
Nor to passions that besmirch
Beauty cherished, spotless and pure.

I offer thee a tear-swept heart
Refreshed as the springtime buds
That saturate the air with fragrance
Sweeping away cold winter's day;
My mind lies in the rainbow's glow
Beside the horizon of its birth
Where love is eternal and deep,
Where thine innocence my soul keeps.

Bring Back My Lover, My Lover to Me

White sails spread against the azure sky,
Come closer, come closer to my sad eyes,
Bring your precious cargo nearer to me
That its great value again I might see:
    Bring back my lover, my lover to me,
    Bring my lover back home to me.

You sailed away long before the dawn,
Sailed away ere the break of morn',
Now wistfully I walk by the roaring sea
Where your sails again I long to see:
    Bring back my lover, my lover to me,
    Bring my lover back home to me.

He kissed me not before he departed;
He left me behind, oh, so brokenhearted;
When he walked into your rolling arms,
He left behind his swashbuckling charms:
    Bring back my lover, my lover to me,
    Bring my lover back home to me.

Alone I walk through the hours of night,
Hoping that he will return with the light,
But all that I hear is the sad moaning sea
Refusing to give back my lover to me.
    Bring back my lover to me, to me.
    Bring back my lover from the sea.

By the shore I sit in the light of the moon,
Heart overcast and chilled by this doom,
Knowing the sea casts its spell over him
As with the ebbtide my hopes grow dim:
    Bring back my lover, to me, to me,
    Oh, you turbulent and heartless sea!

My vigil is over, he does not return,
But on that shore my heart ever burns,
A beacon of hope that the sea will relent
And return a lover to a love never spent:
    Carry my love, you waves of the sea,
    Seek out my lover for me, for me.

The Chalice of Good

A chalice of golden love
Overflowing with the wealth
Poured from a chaste heart
Rests upon a linen-ed altar
Visited by a humble mendicant
Tattered by storms of turmoil.

Where rage the brutal winds
Of despair, howling and frenzied,
Whistling through the rags
Clothing the shivering mind,
Cowed is this poor wretch
Lost in the fens of gloom.

Anoint the mind with sweetness,
Pour out a single drop,
Let spread this sacrament
To halt confusion's rot!

Behold the chalice gleaming,
Within sparkles joyful grace
Blended by austere skill
To serve as the salvation
For him lost in the woods
Where lurk the fretful hours.

Come, beggar, touch thy lips
To this grail now impatient
That the howling gale desist,
And the gloom swiftly depart
Before the calm that falls
As a tapestry of peace.

Enthrall the heart with goodness
That from the chalice spills
Under the eager grasp
Raising it to trembling lips.

See how the storm subsides
And shadows hastily flee,
As the chalice is raised high
From its altar of purity
By the host of seraphims
Come down to blessings bring.

Oh, chalice fair and divine,
In thy tabernacle shrine
With the gifts you consecrate
A soul that now has found
The benediction you sought
To place across its path.

The chalice of golden love
Let fall the silver drop
Upon the mendicant contrite,
Suddenly all despair stops.

When Ends the Toil

Gray marble stands in the twilight's hue
As ghostly sentinels across the night
Vainly seeking to ward off the gloom
That follows swift on silent feet;
And when the burning skies emerge
In storied brilliance to dazzle the sight,
The dismal struggle for the while is lost
Amid the sensuous hours of night.
What bottle pours a better draught
Than starry skies of myriad glows,
Casting warm sparks in darkened realms
And showers lovers' hopes o'er earth?
Not for mortals seems there a design
More perfect with tranquillity divine
Shining as smooth as sequined damask
And mantling all with a velvet touch.
And truth to say many are there
Who have wandered 'neath spangled light
Hearts enraptured or torn by love's breath,
Giddy of sense and shorn of sorrow;
Midnight stars adorn sleeping flowers
Lost in silver shadows of the gardens
Where ambrosia mingles with starlight
And a stolen kiss enhances the hour;
Mortals travel far across the lands,
But the fairest beauty is ever at hand;
Science creates lines and not emotions
Nor fans flames warming lovers' devotion.

'Tis better then to raise weary eyes
Toward distant realms of twinkling light
Where those whose hearts beat as one
Leave gray marble when day is done.

Eternally

When the sun sets beyond the mountains,
    And the stars begin to flicker,
When the moon invades the purple skies,
    And the mockingbird chatters,
    Will you think of me?

When the whitecaps crash upon the shore,
    And seagulls dip and dive,
When the waterfalls thunder aloud and cry,
    While the rapids swiftly fly,
    Will you give a thought to me?

If the world were in my possession,
    And all its wealth were mine;
If songs birds sing belonged to me,
    And they sang from golden trees,
    I would still remember thee.

The world may call me a pure dreamer,
    With ambitions a bit absurd,
But though life's end found me a pauper,
    I would take with me a mind content,
    For your love hath made me rich.

Book Six

Impressions

Impressions

I

When a fair rose grew in December's cold,
  Its fragrance filled the air so bold
Warming frigid days that slowly passed
  While I held its delight close and fast.
It seemed that God had created his best—
  A flower fair surpassing the rest
With beauty dispelling winter's gloom
  Bringing sunlight where snowstorms fumed.
The rose became imprinted upon this heart
  Its wonders overcame me with a start,
Now where footsteps wander I remember
  The fragrant rose that bloomed in December.
Lo, this heart does rejoice and sing
  While the rose changes winter into spring.
Forever will this miracle be mine
  Its wonders food on which to dine
Such strength and courage the rose brings:
  Beauty to life that outgrows all things.

II

Not always does the sun shine in the sky,
  Nor do the stars twinkle merrily on high,
And yet within my heart is a constant glow
  Rocking me in its cradle sweet to and fro;
Angels' voices hum a refrain, a tender lullaby,
  The notes bring gladdened tears to my eyes,

For the music reveals a delight so complete
    Likened to stars when blue heaven they meet.
Whispers softly through halls of my mind,
    Bright lights sparkle within to make me blind,
Through the aura reigns a most heavenly queen
    Who blesses my life with majesty supreme.
So if there are no stars or sun that I may see,
    Still their light shall glow warmly in me,
Oh, infinite is the power flowing in my veins
    With a force that endures and never wanes.

III

Let fall the whitened snow upon the ground
    While in its glory it twirls round and round,
Snowflakes of purity and such soft delight
    Be it in daytime or darkness of night.
The snow will reflect the vast beauty I see
    Which falls from heaven e'er closer to me;
Each snowflake carries an image so dear
    That lounges in this heart with much cheer.
The beauty rests softly within my mind
    Like the snow it dazzles me blind
To the impurities of life lurking on earth,
    For this purity, like snow, hides gristly dirt.
So as lightened footsteps crunch along
    My cleansed heart echoes with a song;
The air becomes filled with incense warm
    Like the rose-scent in the summer's dawn.
And when at night stars on pure snow shine
    The whole world adopts a hue sublime
To fill corners and nooks of my heart
    With purity that shall never depart.

The Desert

Alone in the desert I stand,
It is early morn. Stars palely shine.
The mountains stand like black walls.
The air is cold; I shiver.
The last mournful cry of the coyote trails
The night. A sharp, barking yelp
That fills the air and penetrates my bones.
Cold fingers of ice run down my spine,
    And yet . . .
        The desert! Ridged like strands of rope
        Stretched far beyond my eyes' scope,
        Is not as deathful as it seems
        When cast beneath the pale stars' gleam.
Somewhere I had heard about the desert;
That it was a bleak, still place;
That desolation heavy as the desert sands
Could easily break the spirit of a man;
That there was nothing but brown dullness
And a heavy, morbid silence too;
That it was a friendless waste, empty and vast;
That all was devoured by morbid sands.
    And yet . . .
        The stars that shine upon these sands,
        Are bright enough to light my hands;
        No other place this magic did I find,
        No other stars did my eyes blind.
Already I have seen this evening's stars,
Bright, strong, and swaying magically low;
The brilliant moon was at my fingertips
And the brown dullness turned to silver.
The mountains stood reliefed against the sky,

Dark and black the mountains, deep blue the sky;
No matter where wondering eyes reposed,
Beneath this magic the somberness was lost,
     For . . .
          As I marvelled at the silver moon,
          Quite like the friendly sun of noon,
          My heart and soul were filled with cheer,
          So clean, so good, and oh, so clear.
Now all that seemed dead has disappeared;
Quicksilver and fool's gold touched the sands.
Plainly could I see the hills and tender dunes
While I gazed in admiration at the speckled sky
With its stars of diamonds now so bright,
Now fading at the loss of their magic hue
Tiptoeing reluctantly out of my fond sight,
And bidding farewell to this splendid night.
     And now . . .
          Alone at last in great awe I stand,
          While all of God's magic is at hand,
          Filling my poor soul with great delight,
          Forever banishing my fear of night.
Look! That dreary wall of black breaks,
That solid wall that confined my heart;
Deep purple crowns the mountaintops.
Imperceptibly has this rich mantle formed
And now it spreads itself quite thin.
Where dreariness loomed a glow begins to shine.
The purple touch the fringes of the clouds
Whilst a glorious morn is at hand.
     Alas . . .
          Purple is for the shroud of death,
          For mourning and for deepest regret;
          But purple is also for the advent of morn
          To tell all men another good day is born.

Now the looming mountains become bolder,
As the violets enrichen, then fade, then change
Into maroon and red, crimson and fair blue
And orange, fuchsia, turquoise and yellow too.
See! The mountain crest is bathed in full light;
The weight of darkness is melting fast away.
The soft, fleecy clouds are silver and gold,
Chariots of rich treasures wondrous to behold!
    Ah! . . .
        What wonder it is this radiance to see,
        And to all poor mortals it is free;
        Not a single penny does this wonder cost,
        Not a solitary emotion is 'neath it lost!
At last the fascinating night has fled,
But still its beauty reposes in my mind.
Its miracles echo still. But night is passed,
And delicate morning has approached at last:
And with its advent more delight brings
Works of Nature, never dormant, never still,
To surround my life no matter where I stand
Filling a despairing heart with hopeful hands.
    Yes . . .
        I stand alone amidst the desert sands,
        But all its powers do I now understand.
        There is no longer need for fright,
        Nay! Even the desert is filled with light.

A Strand of Pearls

Look yonder at the lights that glow
    Like pearls upon a strand;
See the flickering gleams on the bay
    That lies smooth as a mirror.
'Tis a bridge, you say, with lights
    To prepare the way for cars,
Yet as I look at them with my eyes
    So full of joy and peace,
They instill within me pleasantries
    Which penetrate my very soul.

Each light is a simple and fair pearl,
    Each one is for a kiss;
And I shall take that gorgeous strand
    And press it to my heart.
And when the cares of day descend
    Upon a sad and weary mind,
Then I shall reflect upon the pearls
    That have become a part of me,
Knowing that forever they shall gleam
    With the brilliance of a dream.

Look! You see the waters ripple!
    The lights now dance and shiver;
But finer is the bright reflection
    That dances on yon waves.
So shall it always be with me
    When a storm may stir and brew,
The pearls shall staunch the roaring
    That strives to inundate me;
And in the darkness shall I see
    The delight you gave to me.

These lights I say are but a sign
  Of something sweeter and fair,
They are the glimmer in your eyes
  And the highlights of your hair.
One by one shall I count these lights
  And change them into pearls;
So that they hang upon this strand
  As though fastened to my hands.
Ever shall they glimmer in the night
  To dispel forever any fright.

Thus I give to thee those lights
  That are strung across the bay;
May they ever guide us through life
  And with ardor light our way.
Until darkness ever shuts them out
  When the doors of life do close,
Until then shall they enlighten
  Our path to sweet repose.
So look now and recall well
  The moments that we shared.

Frost-Bitten Mariner

Frost-bitten mariner on barnacled rock.
Leathery-faced by the lash of the winds,
Watching the gray seas swelling in ire,
Remembering days when seas hummed with calm;
The sweep of the seagull or an albatross glide
In graceful flight o'er a plunging bow
Revives the journey across star-filled seas
That filled your heart with hopes soaring high.

While the rosebush wearied and forlorn,
Somber of color or symmetrical song,
An empty bush with no shadow to cast
Dwells dejectedly upon the past;
Budding flowers must await the dawn
Of springtime with its warmth,
But now all lies in saddened gloom
Friendless beneath the dying moon.

The chilling water with slashing spray
Flies like a whip across the bitten cheeks,
Sending tremors like a million knifepoints
Through the body bent in struggle contrite;
Rushing clouds well in a blackening mood,
Howling winds race across waters that toss,
Plaintively sound the screams of the gulls
Scurrying to vanquish the waves that boil.

Solitude sneaks through woods and dales,
Browned by the cunning of Nature's hands,
Spreading quiet before the fading sun,
Haunted by the brown leaves swirling 'round;

Grayish masses obscure blue skies,
Lowering misery's veil as autumn dies,
Filling the valley with mist and rain,
Vanquishing joy and bringing much pain.

Look to the horizon, a hazy black line
Lost in the struggle of the smashing seas,
Confounded by eyes that seem to be tricked
By the watery blasts unfettered and free;
Perhaps a break will show in the storm,
Forgiving the darkness with hope newly born,
So keep your gaze fastened to the skies
Where hope will spring when storms die.

A whispered song wends through bare boughs
Carried by zephyrs of swiftness and truth,
Leaving behind bleak haunted moments
And floats onward like a white summer cloud;
And the frolicking song of a lost bird
Will whisper its message to sensitive ears
While the hours move on with crafty stealth
Leaving a residue that passes away ne'er.

A Game with Words

What moments are these that in wonderment
    Arouse emotions so vehement?
That awaken a long-lost altruism
    Based upon sincere realism?
It is like the works of an alchemist
    Who within his work insists
Upon a mixture so improvident
    Which results in much astonishment.

Long do I upon great magic reflect,
    And within my own mind project
The delicacy of one so very eloquent
    Who serves ever to supplement
The desires that my whole heart feels
    Aflame with deep burning zeal,
And all that my dreams did prophesy
    Nothing them can ever deny.

Once in my childhood did I lament
    About a great dream misspent,
And so often did I feel remiss
    While sinking into dank abyss
Of despair, that my reason did deride,
    And my senses did divide
Into pain from which I sought influence
    In matters of small consequence.

The years that passed have grown obscure,
    Through them I roamed for a cure
That would bring escape from life's vault
    Which my poor soul might exalt

To pinnacles where I would understand
  What my weary mind commands
And heart prays the world for a mirage
  That my feelings would assuage.

Suddenly from out of the black mist,
  A beautiful image did persist,
Quickly I reached out with eager hand,
  (Oh, I was so very bland.)
To touch the dream now at my reach,
  To implore it and beseech
It to remain with my mind forever,
  There to make fruit of my endeavor.

So there it stood to my great delight,
  My whole being to excite,
The dream was precious upon its throne,
  My long pain did it atone!
For then I knew that my dream was true
  As into my life it flew,
And now once more can I see life
  Unafraid of its murky strife.

The Meadowlark

The meadowlark sang his merry tune,
But his music ended all too soon,
Now echoes stray through dark nights,
Strains pure as stardust bright.
The meadowlark sang a song so gay,
Easing pain on life's sad way;
I strove to comprehend his song
Wafted to me so clear and strong.

Oh, meadowlark! Where do you hide?
Come out that I may stand beside
The beauty of the notes you sing
Blessed with magic of eternal spring.
I did not see you when you sang
The melody that brought such pangs
Within a heart where there now beats
Melancholic throbs without surcease.

Then one evening as I wandered
Across blue seas sprawling yonder,
Your notes I seemed to hear again,
But the song lacked the old refrain.
I walked the chill not knowing where,
Praying the night your song would bare,
All I heard was a springtime breeze
Humming softly through swaying trees.

Meadowlark, meadowlark, return to me,
Enter the gloaming where I may see
The golden throat whistling that tune
Of magic that ended too soon.

Come to warble within this heart
    Stricken since your song departed,
Waft your music as on that first day
    Return and list' to words, I pray.

The little bird far off has flown,
    My prayers to it still unknown,
And gone the wild love that abounded
    When the meadowlark's song resounded.
Someday I hope this warbler returns
    To resurrect a song that burns
Within a heart that since has strayed
    From love the bird carried my way.

Sword of Gold

Take thee the Sword of Gold
In spirit as once was bestowed
A besieged clan, and plunge
Forward with valor in thy hand
To meet the predatory foe
Armored with the devil's might;
And upon the field of battle
With Sword in hand and heart in prayer
Destroy the enemy onto death;
Altho' treacherous foe lurk about thee
Above hovers a mighty ally
Who shall shield thee from harm.
Take up the golden Sword
And with valor in thy hand
Follow righteousness to victory.
Thence sever the head of malice
And the fists of wrong and sin,
Holding them aloft on swordpoint
That others might envision
The triumph of faith and right.

Words

Mayhaps words are ne'er apropos,
For to some words are just words,
To others words form skillful designs
With pattern difficult to discern;
It all depends on the ear that hears,
Thus some words are musical stimulants
Whilst some stir sounds discordant
Which grate painfully on the ear;
The ear may hear a million words
And yet the ear really hears nothing,
But somewhere someone spoke brave words
Which to him loomed dear and precious;
Pause for a moment and recall
What artful play of words words are
When selected with lapidastic care
And matched wtih shining patience;
Yet words are still words, are they not?
And thus they pass through space,
Never halting for fine impressions
And dying somewhere without a trace.

When I Fall Down

I feel this darkness coming on
To grip me in sharpened claws,
Pulling me from this perch I rule
Upon a cloud so pure and soft
    And I fall down
        down
            down.

My mind is swallowed by this gloom,
It fills me with the stench of doom,
Dragging me off into its dank lair
Guarded by gremlins and evils unfair
    As I fall down
        down
            down.

This heart does not strongly beat,
As the world about augurs wrong,
And I am helpless as jetsam wild
Tossed mercilessly on angry brine
    Where I fall down
        down
            down.

Someday perhaps my fall will stop,
And once again I rise to the top,
To sit again upon my soft cloud,
Whence I survey the pit so dark
    Where I fell down
        down
            down.

Book Seven

Dreams

A Broken Dream

Abandoned?
Left in a vacuum of misty memories
To walk the avenues of silence,
The streets of dejection—
Alone.

Abandoned?
By whom that life is a shroud
To blanket corridors of thoughts
And chambers of tranquillity—
Completely.

Alone it seems one wanders
To the horizon without light,
Alone in shattered remembrance
That lies jagged in the mind.

Alone
To collect the pieces of a dream
And patch them into a pattern
That will imprison the past
Forever.

To Believe

To believe in a dream
Until the dream is no more;
Faded and yellowed by time
Captured in the deepest corner
Of a quiet, stilled mind.
To believe in a phantasy
In a world of reality
'Til swatched in a fog,
Shrouded by a stillness
The phantasy is gone.
'Tis to lovers a joy
Vibrant, captured, enduring,
Those moments of dreams
That their souls enslave
To things none understand
Save their hearts.
A dream, elusive, fleeting
Nay! Enduring as time
Rockbound as to the shore
Weathered, but strong
Unfettered, seeking more!
To believe in a dream;
Forever the endless song.
Not filled with fancy
Nor ragged, nor sapped
But filled beyond doubt
With love's tranquil own song.

The Dreamer

Oh, where across what hills and seas
    Hath my eyes dwelt on lovely thee?
Far in the wilderness of my brooding mind,
    Glimmers the sweetness that is thine.

Up into the scraggy hills of wretched life,
    Dispelling all its toils and deep strife,
Enters your beauty, everything to light,
    And chase away the bewilderment of night.

Such are the delights inspired by thee,
    Precious are their tranquil effects o'er me;
To hold you closer and kiss lips that I yearn,
    Ah! How this fire within me burns.

Sweetness and delight, all, and more are thee;
    Shining forth in beauty now and eternally,
Sweeping away all the burdens and my heart console
    With a desire that shall strengthen my soul.

Dreams Are Always Free

Most things in life cost money,
    But dreams are always free,
There is no value placed upon
    The dreams that come to me.
Who can price the moonlit hours,
    Or memories soft and pure?
Who has the wealth to purchase
    The love which hearts endure?

No care have I for silver,
    Give me the stars that shine,
There gleam no dazzling diamonds
    With the flame of stars sublime.
Cast aside the rose-red ruby,
    Its luster dare not compare
With the riches of a stolen kiss
    From lips so chaste and rare.

When wealth has all been counted
    Behind bars and stored to keep,
How can its owner seek to match
    The glow that my dreams reap?
This life is filled with riches
    To be counted one by one,
But dreams live on forever
    Even after the wealth is gone.

Take heed to this wise advice
    Whose wealth kisses the skies,
It does not cost a single pence
    Yet brings joys into your eyes:

Take worthy dreams into your mind,
    And feed them to your heart,
Then set them before your sight
    And cares soon shall depart.

For dreams live on eternal
    With values that ever grow,
No need to lock them in a vault
    You can take them where you go.
No fear is there of robber's stealth,
    Your dreams cannot be stolen,
For though your purse is emptied,
    You're rich in memories golden!

While the World Sleeps

Silently the world sleeps,
Caught in a slumber deep;
Gone are the cares of day,
Quiet are the things to say.

But I? I think of you,
Of sweetness, soft and true,
Filling the darkness of night,
Stopping dreams in full flight.

Softly does your face appear,
Wending in a cloud of cheer,
To fill a heart that ever sings
With joy such as you only bring.

Sleep on, oh, silent world!
Keep tight your dreams unfurled.
I want not your deep quietude;
Nay! She shatters my solitude.

The Dreamer and a Lament

Oh, dreamer! Fled from turmoil and din
    That echoes thunderously o'er life's hills,
What do you see to bring that serene smile?
    Your face is illumined as if by the stars.
Methinks you wander in some mystic paradise
    Where frolic the impish thoughts disguised,
Scented with perfume of elfish hours
    That bloom and die within the mental bower.

Say you life resembles a fragrant garden
    Surmounted by the luster of autumn skies?
Alas! I am blind, possessed not of a single bud
    To intoxicate morbid senses eerily mine.
Tell me, dreamer, tell secrets you hold dear;
    What footpaths of the mind must I pursue?
That this darkness might flee or swiftly fade
    Before the glitter of a fondly sought dream.

Envious are purists lost in the wilderness
    Of thorns and briars twisting on ambitious ground
For they are weary souls who recognize not
    The blueness of the sky nor light of stars;
And I follow through these weeds lost and fatigued
    By the maws of industry enslaving my time,
    While my mind cries out for succor, and my soul
Is marooned in the fens quite dank and drear.

Oh, dreamer! May I join your tranquil fantasy?
    May I intrude the harem of your finest dreams
To become enmeshed in the golden threads
    Which shall guide me into your sublime Eden!

Open, dreamer, the closets of this shallow mind,
Let out the fetid moths spawned of earthy plots;
Replace the darkness with the rainbow's hues
And transport my thoughts to paradise true.

And then, sweet dreamer, wave your magic wand
That I might bask in the sunlight of your mind
Where golden doors of dreams shall open ajar
Before hazy footsteps of a searching heart;
Soothe my soul with music of western winds
And my weariness with lullabies of the seas,
If these you grant, then shall I grow content
No more to blaspheme past days poorly spent.

What Speak I This Eve

If I could whisper but a word—
A solitary word
I'd tell the world about thee,
And the world would rejoice,
But not from what I speak
But from what the world would see;
If all the stars one light combined
And all the jewels bright
Were glistening in the night
Would this be the brightest glow?
Nay, my dear,
Nay, my dear!
There a brighter world must be
Because of the light within thee;
And if I voyaged to the skies
There would I gaze into your eyes.
Let others dream of paradise
Within their earthbound joy,
I have found a sweeter romance
Cradled on heaven's doorstep,
Your beauty is the miracle
To spread God's warmth below,
Your heart is pure as mountain snow
Your smile is a garden rich
But warmer than the summer sun
When blossoms of spring burst forth
To grace my heart with incense
And perfume my soul.
So let me wander in my thoughts
To lands beyond my dreams
To loll on some silken white cloud

My eyes to gaze at thee.
My dearest one,
My fairest one,
What speak I this eve?
I pray reveal your loveliness
Hath come my life to bless.

When Rose Petals Fall

This heart misses you as do daisies
    Pleading for the noonday breeze,
Or the green carpets spreading far
    Yearn for the kiss of morning dew.
My soul is empty as the tempest
    When the wind has lost its rage,
And my mind is as black as evening
    Without the elixir of the stars.

I miss you with all the fervor
    Of flaming bonfires soaring high,
Or the orange mellowness of a taper
    Once flickering fires sigh.
I miss the sparkle of your heart
    So soft as dawnbreak's gleam,
For the longing in my possession
    Is the ember lighting my dreams.

I miss you with the loneliness
    Of a poet wandering in prose,
Or the sadness that comes lingering
    When petals fall from the rose.
The blessings that my heart counts
    Are many when you are near,
But they vanish with the footsteps
    Of departure's haunting fear.

Garden of Your Love

Today, you walk as in the past,
Tomorrow dawn breaks anew,
Life forever will be altered
Freshened by sweeter dew;
Grace your life well, I say,
With contentment and full bliss,
Blest with godly splendor
By magic of a midnight kiss;
The sun will rise o'er your lives,
Amber goodness shineth bright,
May all the wonders of this day
Through all hours be your light;
Content and with new courage
Enter Valhalla of sweet joy
Let overflow the cup of happiness
That with majesty mantles all.

So when dawn does break anew
May plans as starlight glow,
Atop yon silver tree of magic
In glens where joyness flow;
Your pathway lies before you
Your life by heaven planned
As upon earth you are guided
By an unseen caring hand;
Let your heart in tender smile
Reveal all that you hold near
For in each other's presence
Blossoms life precious and dear;
And in all your quiet hours,
Let the memories in sweet scent

Fulfill the garden of your love
With fragrance never spent.

A Journey to Heaven's Skies

Together we shall climb the stairway
That leads us to the stars,
I'll take your hand,
I'll take your heart
And lead it to that light;
And there we'll rest
On the rainbow's breast
To gaze at the earth below,
To watch the humans scamper
As through this life they go;
And when the stardust glitters
Upon yon heart I love,
I'll know it's in safekeeping
Of sweetest angels above;
So take yon heart
And take yon hand
As we enter our promised land,
Soon I'll walk beside you
As we travel through the blue
Into our bright paradise;
We shall loll in azure grandeur
Of quiet celestial splendor
While moonbeams glaze avid eyes;
How sweet this wonder
Amid all the fragrance
Wafting from garden's flora.
The angel will come
With her magical wand
To gild our hearts with love;
Oh! Lovers shall flee
On shafts of the stars

Into an ethereal trance;
What sweet romance
Shall come to our hearts
As from earth we depart;
Together we shall climb the stairway
To wander amid the stars,
Please take my heart,
Please take my soul,
Ne'er pause in earthly flight,
And atop that rainbow
Shall repose our souls
Far from the worldly toils,
So it will matter not
If the present is forgot,
For our love has reached its goal;
Amid the stars shall we recline
Swathed sublime
In the presence of heaven's glow.

The Weaver of Dreams

Where children's laughter rings without end,
In the land of magic and wonder,
Where leprechauns leap in joyful frenzy
Enters the mind when lost in dreams.
Into the miracles of thoughts that shine
With the glimmer of lighthouse beacon,
Penetrating the fog of daily living,
Passes the traveller covered with sleep.

Down the silvered road that meanders
Toward the castle where there dwells,
The little king so impish and proud
Who creates realities with star-tipped wand.
Oh, sleeper! Drowse on through the night
In your thoughts of magic to come,
Wander quietly through halls of your mind
Where you become a part of your dreams.

The royal man reigns from a throne of clouds,
Supported by the silver of the moon,
Led to by a pathway from the golden sun
That passes beneath the rainbow's arch.
Crowned is he with a tiara of lost dreams,
Sprinkled with jewels of fond hope,
Mantled by the velvet of pleasant schemes,
He revels in the aspirations of one's dreams.

His face is impish with sweet desires
That have set all dreamers afire,
While in his deep eyes twinkles the joy
Of fulfilled dreams by man fiercely sought.

Wrinkled are his cheeks from ambitions
That grow stealthily in the warped minds
Which he staunchly tries to resist
And replace with dreams more sublime.

Ah! Now he beckons; who shall respond?
The dreamer wafts across the room
And bows profusely before this kingly one
Who knows what thoughts spin in the mind.
Come, speak up! What shall you wish?
Money? A yacht, or some rare trinket?
A home? A sweetheart, an auto or a ranch?
Maybe a palace with a ballroom of gold
Where slavish dancers sway to and fro?

Yes, all these things may come to you,
Though only in dreams will they be true,
Still they do bring moments of great joy
That fill the heart with a feeling warm.
So dream on amid the pomp and circumstance
Which is yours in the serenity of night,
Fear not to fill your mind with silver dust
Of dreams that will echo through your life.

The little king watches and knows
As his button nose shines with a glow
Of moonlight that blushes and radiates
With the fondness for loved ones below.
He takes the stardust in a jeweled bowl
And sprinkles it with the rays of pure gold
That spring forth from the wondrous sun,
All magical in its radiance so bright.

And then he takes the dawn so clean,
Matches it with the twilight's scene,
And lo! The dreamer passes through his dreams
Surrounded by nature's most astute beams.
Now he takes the raindrops so clear,
Laves the mind 'til it is filled with cheer
As crystalline as the kindly moon
Which vanquished the sorrow of night's gloom.

Oh, filled with tricks is the little man,
A wave of the wand, a gesture of the hand
Makes everything pleasant to understand;
He clears out the gloom, brings the warmth
Of sunshine where had raged storms,
While 'neath the pallid summer skies
Blessed with the fragrant delight
He casts off the evils of fright.

The dreamer stirs with a smile on his face,
His forehead is covered with a trace
Of magic spellbound in his thoughts
By the ruler of the castle in the sky;
He opens his eyes and does still see
The path that to the impish throne led,
Lost in the heavens where there resides
The weaver of dreams our lives to guide.

Book Eight

Revelations

Revelation

I find that I must sing again
    Of sweetness and delight,
Of sprightly birds and flowers
    And silver stars of night;
The moon lights up the gloaming
    Snows shimmer on the hills;
The sun lightens blue waters
    Whilst kissing daffodils;
Methinks I need croon anew
    Of joyful moments bright,
Of angelic face and pure heart
    Through hours of sublime light.
Across the warm summer lanes
    Reposed by waters gay,
Where moonglow paints the night
    With stars across the bay.
To sing of nature is endless,
    For her miracles are not few,
To dream is seeking refuge
    In the reveries old and new;
Still beauty of dear nature
    Is naught compared to thine,
And sunsets and sunrise
    Are never more divine.
I find within my eager heart
    A magic gay and sweet,
With images of soft beauty
    Never bitter, always neat.
Let celestial bodies glitter
    And let summer breezes blow,
What care I for ocean spray

Or frolic where I go?
Indeed the golden sunshine
    Though warm and soft and pure
Is but dying embers
    When matched with love demure.
Sing happy songs and parodies,
    Extol odes towards skies
For there can nary be
    Songs joyful as thine eyes,
Nor winds awhisper in the trees,
    Nor brooks humming along
To murmur of the loveliness
    A stranger to any wrong.
So as my footsteps pass away
    And night falls mercilessly,
Let the echoes of a poor heart
    Be your poetic melody.
And when my eyes again return
    Upon your visage fair,
I'll know as every star knows
    An angel is standing there.

The Gods at Work

The gods brought you down, brought you down,
The gods brought you down from the sky;
You came enthroned in a bower like a queen,
Enthroned upon a cloud silvered and agleam.
The heavens were flaming and stars did glitter,
The moon sparkled wisely while bluebirds flitted.
The gods placed you proudly on a carpet of gold,
Placed you down for the wide world to behold.
And your beauty was a miracle to see
From the heights of mountains, soft depths of the sea.
The roses knelt gently at your wee tender feet,
Knelt in entrancement at perfection complete.

The stars pined for the glory of your eyes,
Pined demurely and wanly at your sparkling fire;
The moonglow danced and shimmered in your hair,
Quivered and shivered before your beauty so rare;
Then the gods smiled and crowned you with delight,
Knowing the earth's sinners would witness your light.
Then took they in hand the incense of heaven,
Took it and sprinkled it for goodness to leaven;
When they were done molding this sculpture so pure
With a symmetry for the cherubims to lure,
Softly they sped off to castles nestled so high,
Sped away to take more treasures from the sky.
Coyly they returned, returned from their goal,
Returned with blessings to penetrate your soul;
Your heart they filled and dusted with silver,
Filled it so fully that in darkness it glimmered;
A smile did they give, did they give with song,
And sang out gaily at this miracle sans a wrong;

Proudly they spread wings for a gay journey home,
A journey completed beneath the sky's azure dome;
And now that the gods have returned to the blue,
They look down with favor upon your beauty so true,
And in fickleness they sent for a minstrel to view
This delight that he might song sonnets about you.

Olympic Idols

Two goddesses on Mount Olympus peer out
Across the fleecy fields of white,
And through swift-closing rifts
Gaze at the sprawling sights below
So distant from their own time,
So wrought with change that changes—
And they sought to understand it all.
Couldst one explain
That time incessant alters time
Whilst seas of green ne'er leave their shores?
Upon yon mount' where Delphic oracles spoke,
Where alabaster columns o'er gray ruins rise
Bathe' by myriad light the scene unfurls,
Each panorama a drama on the craft
Of hours; where Aeolus plotted with Ares
To sweep across ancient Athens, Athens new,
Thence to flee to Aegean seas where Pegasus roved,
There turned the gazes from the timeless hill.
Eros in her white cultist drapes,
Half nude with delicate, full breasts,
Whose shapely form enticed her race
Still stands seductive and mysterious
As if to search the truths within her mind
Whilst hollow eyes mocked hidden secrets
Of trysts where sins in her name sprang—
Those moments when lovers embraced
As one amid the downy passion of love,
Casting off the raiments woven by hands,
To rest unveiled in sensualities sublime;
But Agape demure less boldly clad,
Nor sophisticate with vacillating trends

Mutely stands; yet soft-chiselled visage
Reflected signs of victory over matters
Placed first in minds of woman and man
By Eros; the twain on Mount Olympus were foes
Locked in struggle for souls of man.
Where Mount Olympus looks towards the sea
And ancient Athens in dead glory basks,
Which of these two is sweeter?
The one to intermingle bodies as one
Or the other minds to commingle forever
In the eternal wonders of a paradise
Where passion is a fruit of souls
And not of body. Oh, snared betwixt the two
Like puppets congregate their clans,
Succored by the white grace of Agape
Or stunned by the hot fires of Eros,
On the seething lea sown in lovers' minds.
Two goddesses indeed in cold silence stare
Outward across the fluctuating mass;
Which idol seekest thou? The one to capture
Moments which pass and stir faint sparks,
Or the other which emblazons moments
Which endure to stir flames to the skies?

Artemis

I am the moon of yellow or gold—
I am the silver disc of winter cold,
Or the warm mellowness of love;
I am the moon.

Tell me then, O moon on high
What seeth thou in thy journey?
Tell me the tales lovers spin
Or the sagas men of envy create.

I am the moon—speak I of all
That passed before my light,
'Twould need the years to come
And shut me out of the night;
Yet I can tell you of many things,
Of songs that minstrels sing
To loved ones beyond their reach;
Of epic tales recounted vividly
To engrossed lads of tempted age.
Yet to me the many matters I see
Are nothing, tho' something they seem,
And compared to one moment
Of lost paradise, nothing is everything.

O yonder moon, weave a path
Fixed by mightier hand than thou,
Still you play words and tones
And speak not with that clarity
Which thy light cleaves in heaven;
'Tis better to remain silent
Save to recount the tales so soft

Spun of silver light and stars
Into a tapestry of immaculate design,
And this damask is suspended
With invisible strands and bonds
Woven from the warm emotions
From palpitating heart. I am the moon—
For lo, these million years
My light has been cast on earth
And all the years wrenched
From moldy calendars reflect not
What filled the hours of each day;
But ere I reach the zenith
And my light becomes lost,
Let my aged existence
Fill in the void of aching pain;
Simply, I may reveal an ode
To wit: In paradise created are
     The marvels of all life,
     In gilded chariots of gold
     The marvels pass my eyes;
     Many have I seen, many more
     Shall my aged light reflect,
     But of all the marvels I see
     Only one can I call perfect;
     A billion stars in the heavens
     Each shedding its bit of light,
     Form a crown of dancing gems
     Atop the head of night;
     More wondrous than all this,
     A diadem of flaming white,
     The matchless soul of pureness
     Swathed in heaven's might;
I am the moon.
And this I say to you,

Light follows darkness and reversed,
Darkness by light is shattered,
For each tremor opaque
A glow of warmth is assured;
Seek ye then the epitome of mind
Creating a vision adorned
In the image of what you seek,
And it shall come as light comes
That the perfection sought
Was ever present, ever near,
As close as thine own heart.

No Time for Despair

Creatures who trod this earth
Infinite in their moods and whims,
Take the brightness from each day
To curdle it in different ways;
They rankle starlight with dire cries
Corrupting wonders of the skies.

If man opted to look around,
To study the world wherein he resides,
If he took a moment to count his gifts,
He would uncover the greatest peace
Rises from a source beyond his reach.

This lesson learned tho' it were hard,
That others' woes are worse than mine;
If I think the world is of great weight,
Then I am blind and unwilling to see
A friend burdened with problems so large
Which reduce mine to lilliputian size.

If the day is dark when it you greet,
Then cross to the other side of the street,
For surely there you will come to find
A meaning to life ever more sublime;
And if darkness about you persists,
Its pernicious grip strive to resist.

When clouds seem to roll into your life,
When all about you is wrought with strife,
When all you feel is wickedness about,
Seek a balm that will soothe your mind;

Look yonder towards stars so bright
Twinkling, twinkling o'er the night.

If shoulders burdened are with care,
If you see dismal failure about,
If footsteps grow weary and drag
Turn to unseen founts of strength;
About you are many fine things,
Inspiring you to shout and sing.

Though life may seem a hopeless task,
Though all you meet are schemes and greed,
Though everywhere lie hate and despair
Reach for the goodness teeming inside
Since all creatures have virtues fine
When caused to sparkle, make life sublime.

So what if tears roll down your cheeks,
So what if your mind is sadly uneased,
So what if you think it's a one-sided race,
A time there comes when you'll be more gay;
Reach into man for a piece of God's warmth
For it is in man since the time he was born.

Knowest Thou a Moment Still

Knowest thou a moment still
When time paused in flight
And seas lay calm while stars
Shone bright? Knowest thou
The aspen heart and placid mind
Lulled by perfumed morphic winds
Into an erotic trance?
A wink of an eye, a star's flicker,
The echo in the hills, all these
A moment own and then gone away
No more to be, no more to stay;
The fringe of day meeting the night,
That thrill born of an incident
Pause not nor linger more,
Vanishing swift as the rainbow's light.
Yet knowest thou a moment is
A year, an eon, an eternity?
It descends in pompous splendor
To reign its fleeting paradise,
Then passes on; but behold its mark
Ageless as time on stolid hills,
Fathomless as the ocean depths,
Seared in the mind to be born again
Without end 'til the end itself;
A moment, a year or an eternity,
What paradox of words! Nay,
Not the guile of aimless speech
But the wisdom of an inner mind,
Reviving the beauty as of yore
Whose soul-flames embrace the warmth

Which unlocks the doorway of the past
To admit refreshing memories.
  A moment given in the shelter
  Of a soul where no umbrage dwells,
  Where glistens heaven's gold
  Burnished in purity ever virgin;
  A moment escaped from burdens
  Of soiled hours, filled with nectar
  Sweeter than Bacchus' sweet brew
  Poured from a grail of white;
  A moment spared to a tired heart
  To hasten its beat and to restore
  The knowledge of the chaste care
  Which graces it evermore.
Who casts aside the purity
Of a moment divine in being
Tho' confined to the metronome
Of time escaped to eternity?
Not I nor anyone whom fortune
Caressed with a garden's fragrance
Where blossom the moments rare
Sought by hearts in loving quest;
Poor fools who wander aimlessly
Restrained from just reward,
For granted once the priceless gift
They sensed not its pure wealth;
The vision scans obscure horizons
And fastens to transient things,
A stranger to what it sought
The essence of its marvels lost;
But better the one who has found
If but briefly the beauty awesome,
Which piercing the mind there abides
Adorned in a precious moment's pride!

Book Nine

Canticles

Canticles

I

Stars that shine brightly in soft summer skies
Shed pale light upon hearts in great search
For tranquillity in this world of chaos and dogma
So that peace will descend upon one's soul.
Looking aloft at the twinkling diamonds fair
There comes to mind a goddess beyond compare,
Who reigns the spacious heavens with sweetness
And looks benignly upon an ambitious slave.
In awe do I whisper chords enchanted and deep-felt
Trusting the breezes will waft them to her
Hoping that listening she will look down and smile
And thus uplift my sad and desolate heart.
For a smile from her is radiant as sunbeams,
As fragile and sweet as a soft summer breeze,
As tender and enchanting as a mother's hymn,
That fills the air as the stars paint the sky.
So do I pray through these hours of strife
Unspoken thoughts that seek ever to reveal
Secrets of heart and a search for life's treasure
From one whose dearness does bring pleasure.

II

The storm clouds gather, glum and dark,
    Shattering the light 'cross the sky;
The lightning flashes, thunder rolls,
    Bleak darkness blinds my eyes.

Who can understand the cause of this,
    Perhaps a word or innocent sign;
Yet the mind is clouded with despair,
    To which inner battle is resigned.
But after the storm the light reappears,
    Again the world glitters bright.
The clouds roll off into another scene
    Leaving behind a beauteous, clear night.
Ah, the moments when the storm lasts,
    Bring naught but sorrow and fear;
For it dispels the magic in your heart
    As burning eyes rain desolate tears.
I wait for that sun to shine once more,
    In hopes that it will bathe me
With the brilliance of an endless grace
    Which dark clouds had tried to erase.

III

Where is that eternal light that shines
    Above the earthly toil and brine,
To reach deep within my heart to bare
    The wondrous miracles of your care?
For me, who wretchedly travels life,
    Fulfilling all daily dues and strife,
Must ever stop to beg for sweet scents
    Which stop my plunge into fiery descent.
It is you I seek, as I would starlit sky,
    Yearning for the glow residing in your eyes;
For precious it is, and much dearer too
    To ask for delights brought only by you.
How nice to stop e'er the while to reflect,
    Upon dearest you, adorable and perfect,

Who brings contentment wherever you go,
    But especially within my poor helpless soul.
So stay awhile and sate me with your nectar
    Which dissolves and dissipates all cares,
Then shall I travel lighter on life's road,
    With burdenless toil and enlightened load.

IV

Let me open my eyes to see life,
    As it lies sprawling, brawling before me;
So that I may look upon all the strife
    Without any prejudice or bias.
Let me delve deeply into this pool
    That is endless, deep, yet confused,
So that this desolation I can lose
    And of life I will never tire.

V

Darkness falls and with it brings gloom,
    Like the clutches of an impending doom;
For the black void will take you away,
    And bring the close to another sad day.
Then I must seek within my silent mind,
    An elixir of joy revived by memory mine,
Which shall dissolve this dank and fetid mood,
    That ever haunts my poor soul which broods.
Oh, let me seek and find your tender smile!
    Shatter this darkness, linger yet awhile,
So that this worn heart can have its sought fill
    Of the eternal longing to kiss you still.

Let me hold your hand in a contented dream,
  'Twill shatter despair 'neath mellow moonbeams;
To touch your lips so like the sunkissed dew,
  Fills my heart as stars fill the blue.
Such sweetness fair you only can impart,
  Come, come, sweet one, and fill this heart
With joyful song, and with fond delight,
  Only then will gloom flee the grasp of night.

VI

Infinite is time as it passes us by,
  Yet time is not as strong as my heart,
Which beats swiftly for a touch divine,
  Pressed sweetly from your lips on mine;
The world has gazed upon many sights,
  But this wonder that glows in the night,
Lies uncovered as a gem clear to behold,
  By those whose eyes dare to be bold.
So time, when you pass through the hours,
  Hold still that moment wherein flowered,
The fragrant delight of two hearts demure
  That beat with feeling wonderfully pure;
And in my thoughts will time ever last
  With its great joy o'er a delightful repast,
When hungry heart and flushed lips met
  While caring eyes with glad tears were wet.
Time then will hold no fear for you or I,
  We have passed from this earth into the sky,
Where we gaze on each other as do the stars
  Upon lovers so near, and yet so far.

VII

When darkness swallows the thoughtful mind
　　And gloom pervades the heart,
What sedative does my being yearn to find,
　　Which will make such sadness depart?
Thoughts turn to one who in regal splendor
　　Reigns within the sorrower's dreams;
And enters his despair with warmth so tender,
　　That darkness need flee, it seems.
She comes demurely, daintily with fairness,
　　Face a-glistening as the autumn sun,
Her smile so sweet wafts o'er me like a caress,
　　Which apace makes the gloominess to flee.
Fondly then reach I beauty to touch,
　　To gaze at her with eyes intent,
To know that she understands feelings, and such,
　　And then only is my being content.
The blackness dispels itself and light does shine,
　　Brilliance aglow everywhere spatters;
Misery engulfing me departs, all is fine,
　　Because you answered my prayers.

VIII

As majestic as the snow-draped mountains,
　　And wondrous as the budding trees;
Beautiful like the gentle rolling seas,
　　Or the tanager singing gaily on yon tree.
All these art thou, and even prettier still,
　　With a beauty that ever brings a thrill.
To look at thee is to gaze at starry skies,
　　And watch full moon enthroned on high;

The rainbow with deft and brilliant hues,
  Is like a halo crowning thy fair head;
The sun that shines so brightly o'er the earth,
  Sparkles not as brilliantly as thy face.
And harvest-ripened plains spread afar,
  Lose magic when thy lips in smile do part,
No fairer one has trod across worldly stage,
  None other ever captured thy tender grace
Which penetrates a heart that does ever see,
  The tranquil beauty that is all of thee.

IX

What makes man's mind undergo such change
And why must man become so glum?
These clouds that roll across the mind
Are like the denizens of the slums.
For my mind becomes an animal of despair,
It sinks to the guttered level,
I turn and turn possessed with great fright
As I seek to escape this mad devil.
Yet in turmoil my mind does hold fast
To a fragile straw that will succor me;
She stands apart, bathed in bright light
That seeks and seeks to set me free.
Who can withstand the roseate warmth
Of an angel sent this heart to hold?
One who will lift me from the storm's throes
And tenderly to her bosom me enfold.
So though I sink into the maws of gloom,
Dark though it may always be,
Somewhere in the heavens reigning above
Is that sweet angel guarding me.

X

Let alone the schemes that rule all men,
    And concentrate on matters of heart;
To others leave the dogmas and rules,
    Whilst you seek joy of fine living.
Look toward the one who in delight brings,
    Sweetness of soul and peace of face,
Contain her beauty in your heart which knows
    She defeats the cares of day.
Hold fast to knowledge her presence brings,
    Unmask pagan idolatry, replace it with her,
So that the mind grows more content.
    Silently into your thoughts she will enter,
To cast off the barnacles of despair;
    She tramples down the thorns and burrs,
Replacing them with scented roses.
    And wherever you be, she accompanies thee,
Revealing glorious byways of the heart;
    The path grows less steep and easier to tread,
For she will carry thee on her wings.

XI

There is such great fright in my life,
    That you might turn from me;
And then I would sink into much despair,
    Because you would not be there.
And oh, such darkness comes upon me,
    When this thought I entertain,
Suddenly all of life seems useless,
    And my struggles all in vain.
Say that you will e'er be with me,

In my mind and in my heart;
That no matter where this life leads us,
We will never be apart.
And if these words you do utter,
My heart would thus be thrilled,
For then my dark fears are nothing,
Since you are with me still.
So tell me this fright of mine
Is but a passing thing;
Words to this effect would be joy
And my dream anew would sing.

XII

The cries of anguish that torment the soul,
Submerge a heart that cannot find,
Tranquillity amidst the rabble of the world
Which stifles and chokes its growth.
And then I turn towards a hope, perhaps,
Somewhere there will be a ray
Of light which will lift me up above the crowd
Towards a knowledge that this torment
Is unwarranted and therefore within this life
There may be some semblance of peace
Which will pacify the tumultuous destruction
Taking place inside and corroding
The mind until crazed with improper despair
An end to all the struggle is sought.
Yet it is not we who must decide this question
For it is beyond our scope and reach;
So onward one continues, against great odds,
That handicap and confuse the soul.

XIII

There springs within the heart gratitude
 For the efforts which you show
Towards a tormented soul, sunk in despair
 Which cannot understand this life;
In all its entirety; and in its malcontent
 Must continue against the world
Woe to this heart if your kindness melted away!
 For it would be the blackest day,
And life would become a festered, sordid thing,
 Which would rive the heart in two.
Knowledge of your presence and tenderness
 Serves to pacify the wretched soul;
The understanding and the care you bring
 Are soothing to this mendicant.
For thou are salve upon the gaping wounds
 Of life which suffocate and choke
And me reduce into a melancholic state
 Who stands naked of achievement.

XIV

Oh, heart! So filled with tumultuous beatings,
 Release thy emotions and throb content;
Pass off the devils lurking in confusion there,
 Allow the joy of living to hold its sway.
Reach for the inspiration that will lift you
 Above and beyond the sins of mortal man;
Entrust to this deity the path of your life,
 To guide you safely through the briared lanes.
Place thy hopes and thy dreams into her hands
 So that she will mold you into the future,

A dreamer with ambition filled and achieved,
Whose golden words and silvered phrases,
Extol her wondrous influence upon thee;
Such that the world's natural gifts
Become thine to give to her with all thy care.
And heart, forget never that these endeavors
Become a part of thee when her face fills dreams
That tormented thee through wearied hours.
And if this you remember, then all thy success
Will bless thee in flowered bower.

XV

When the world is shrouded in darkness
And the sun no longer shines,
Man will for one thing be thankful
For the sweetness that is thine.
Your laugh will make the stars sparkle,
And your voice will make bells ring,
A glance from you is a proud possession
For to me it means everything.
How can there be gloom in the world
When you are near and about?
Since to gaze upon thy fair sweetness
Ever wants my heart to shout?
Thus will I raise my voice in refrains
Of the delight you bring to me;
And I hope the whole world awakens
To the love you are to me.

XVI

For then would flare such a passion
As was never seen before
And the magic of her touch the key
To bring him into paradise,
And content was he that she
Was the vessel to carry him there.
And she? Was she content to be subject
To the flame that them devoured?
Her beauty was fuel to fan the flames
Of passion and make them soar higher,
And he was spent with the fervor
With which he sought to possess this beauty;
She remained silent and he despaired
Profound indeed that she cared not,
And yet he was not certain, for she
Was not passive, but sought the gates
Of paradise herself, and found them
In his arms; thus they embraced
Cast upon the downy clouds of love
Far from the sullies of the earth,
Until passion expired and lo!
'Twas never passion but strange love.

XVII

Art thou burdened as the ass with faggots
And toil fraught with futile despair?
Is thy mind frozen with winter blasts
Shaping a thousand mental needles
Which in sharpened pain cause outcries
Decrying the bounds wherein you trod?

But let me humbly come to bring a petal
From a flower reposed in rich bouquet,
That its fragrance might dispel the drear
And wretched thoughts, and thus cleansed
You may wander down a primrose path;
For troubles weighty though they seem
Are but clouds that understanding dispels;
So let this light in tenderness warm
Suffuse your mind and thus uncover
That what today was a burden deep
Is but a ripple that swift' fades away,
And in the aftermath your heart will view
Waters of life placid as a summer lake
Stirred by more pleasant hours; and life
Will be enriched, for thus have you found
The infinite magic of peace of mind.

XVIII

Beyond the mind lies greater beauty
    If one would dare to seek it;
This wonder that before the eyes unfolds
    Such secrets of the heart and soul.
A deity stands regally upon her throne
    With smile so sweet and tender,
Stars sparkle in her kindly and dear eyes,
    Shedding myriads of brilliance o'er me,
Her face is soft and delicate as the moon,
    Which reigns majestically on high;
This deity stands in aura of pure delight
    Watching on a struggling being,
Who implores her to guide and inspire him
    With her goodness and enraptured light.

For my prayers speed upward towards her,
In a gesture of hope and care,
That she will listen to matters I implore
With acceptance and a caring heart.

XIX

The sun rises like a golden crown
Atop yon lofty mountain;
It climbs the skies without a sound
Towards its celestial throne.
From whence I gaze it comes to me
That you are like that sun,
You grace a hallowed throng within
And make all my cares run,
Thou art a queen regal and fair
Who rules the world I reside;
You make my doting eyes to stare
Upon thy beautiful face.
And all through life I shall gaze
Upon the memories you impart;
You will wander ever down the trail
That leads straight to my heart.

XX

The stars that flicker in the evening sky
Hardly compare with the magic of your eyes
Which cast their glow on this joyous soul
Who seeks to bask unending in their light.
For thou art a celestial being from above,
Come to bring peace upon a weary heart,

And you have entered with sweetest delight,
Of my being to become an inspiring part,
Fair are the skies, but fairer is your smile,
Sweet is the clover, but sweeter are your lips,
Majestic are the mountains but more so your heart,
Peaceful are the waters of life you give.
Contented forever shall this soul ever be,
Refreshed by the miracles pouring from thee,
Where I may turn, your face will shine fair,
And in my thoughts thy image dearly cherish.
Never to roam a moment without recalling thee,
Not one footstep to take without seeing you,
Not a solitary mile will pass beneath my feet
Without my recalling this angel from the blue.

XXI

Sometimes when the sun goes down,
The smile is replaced by a frown;
Yet, though outwardly there is gloom,
For contentment within there is room;
It matters not if the world is dark,
Or whether one walks alone in the park,
There is something finer in the day,
And perhaps it will come your way.
Adopt anew that saving smile,
Which will stay with you all the while;
Take a glance at the world about
And in joy you may strive to shout;
For after darkness there comes light
As surely daytime follows night,
So look ahead to a happier hour
When happiness again will flower.

XXII

I waken to the trill of birds
Whose notes form an angel's song:
The melody followed where'er I go
With sweetness bound me as thongs.
Through hours of daily lassitude
Within me echoes that melodic song,
Beating and pulsing through my veins,
Averring that no notes are ever wrong.
As in silence I pause to ponder
From whence the music does come
With a flash the mind clears quickly
For the song streams from the sun.
But not that sun one views each day
This sun bursts dazzling and fair,
For as I search to find the tune
I discover that you are there.

XXIII

You think that I would forget
Memories you give to me?
Or that my mind is fickle
Discarding hours with thee?
Nay! One cannot blot the sun,
Nor do away with content',
You have blessed a weary heart
With perfumes of heaven's scent.
You richly glide into my life
Like clouds a-sailing in the sky,
No matter where I hap' to turn
You blossom rich before my eyes.

Fear not that I seem full of haste
Or my actions bring a start,
Remember ever this, I say
You are the jewel of my heart.

XXIV

The rill wending over green turtles' backs,
Squirrels, chipmunks as walnuts they crack,
All of these and more do I sense—
The little white house with white picket fence,
Covered with roses and sparkling with cheer
Of soft cries and echoes of loved ones dear.
To my sense there grows in a bright row
Tall wheat, golden-shafted, row on row;
The wheatfields and prairies, the hills and the vales
A sacred white church a-snug in the dale.
All of these wonders float before eager eyes
That silently watch while quietly I lie.

XXV

How nice to sit, on a soft summer night,
In darkness aglow with firebugs' light,
Inhaling the passion of honeysuckle rose
As its perfume upon soft breezes blows.
And quiet the night beneath flickering stars
While I gaze intently hither and afar,
Basking in memories of a silvery hue
Falling upon me like yon moon in the blue.
All is serene now, many things do I see
The birds in the forest, the ants and the bees,

The cornfields in summer, the woodlands of fall,
The rivers so deep and the mountains so tall.

XXVI

Were I to stand disconsolate in points unknown,
    And around me lay great desert wastes,
My mind would wander over the swirling dunes,
    To find its way to you in much haste.
For no matter where this soul should travel,
    Be it on the vast land or mighty sea,
My heart would ever seek to return again
    To its place beside and within thee.
It does not count if the miles should spread
    Between two persons with beating hearts,
That achieve contentment in being together,
    And which feel great anguish when apart.
So while we may let us smile, talk, and laugh,
    Let our hearts be etched upon our eyes,
Let our lips meet sweetly in a kiss divine,
    And together we'll leave this valley of sighs.

XXVII

Distance is something that is measured by man,
    Something tangible, easy to understand,
But distance can never in all its great gloom
    Sever this light that shines in the room
Where my heart may be; and though absent you are
    And the distance between us keeps us apart,
You shall be beside me, so close and so near
    That never again shall I wallow in fear

Instead, I shall dream of delights that you brought,
   Overcoming inner conflicts I stubbornly fought.
Over me shall come sensations sublime
   Defining everything as mighty and fine.

XXVIII

Mighty and fine—ah—how wonderful this is;
   This feeling that all of my mind and heart fills.
How glorious! As beautiful as the rising sun
   Wholesome and delightful as all artistry done;
This emotion that can top the world's highest peak,
   That never fills depths and for which I ever seek,
The wonderful delicacy that comes from knowing you,
   A feeling sincere, awesome, deliciously true!
My heart overflows when upon you my gaze rests
   Obscuring the gloom, enlightening all that is best.
My soul grows joyful, to the heavens it flows
   Since my heart alone owns this feeling I know.

Epilogue

This Second

This second
Knifes between the past and present;
This second
Is now.
This second
Is life.
Yesterday is dead,
Tomorrow is unknown;
This second
One must live.
The past cannot return,
The future lies unhastened;
This second
Is the present.
Cling to it for its value
And its delight,
In a twinkling it will vanish
And be no more.

Alone

If importance, lust or rancor
    Fill your heart as buzzing bees,
Stop, reflect a moment,
    Be more of what you should be.

If you find you're growing greedy,
    And avarice is nigh,
Take a look into a mirror,
    Be little less of what you are.

If you think the world's against you
    And things seem to go awry,
Be more of what you should be,
    A little less of what you are.

When the whole world seems appalling,
    And you're steeped in misery,
Be less of what you are,
    A little more of what you should be.

Alone one cannot wander,
    Alone one cannot stand;
Be a servant to all mankind,
    Stretch out your helping hand.

Be Proud

Be proud . . .
    Of your God
    Your country
    Your blood
    And your family, too.

Show your pride . . .
    In your eyes
    Your heart
    Your smile
    And your words, too.

If angered . . .
    Show your anger as the sea
    Pounding you from without
    But let it not pass
    The shoreline of your mind.

Be glad . . .
    You are alive
    The air is free
    Your thoughts are pure
    And love is yours to keep.

Index